Frederick Denison Maurice

The Claims of the Bible and of Science

Correspondence between a Layman and the Rev. F.D. Maurice on some Questions

Arising out of the Controversy Respecting the Pentateuch

Frederick Denison Maurice

The Claims of the Bible and of Science
Correspondence between a Layman and the Rev. F.D. Maurice on some Questions Arising out of the Controversy Respecting the Pentateuch

ISBN/EAN: 9783337306984

Printed in Europe, USA, Canada, Australia, Japan

Cover: Foto ©Lupo / pixelio.de

More available books at **www.hansebooks.com**

THE
CLAIMS OF THE BIBLE

AND OF

SCIENCE.

CORRESPONDENCE.

BETWEEN

A LAYMAN AND THE REV. F. D. MAURICE

ON SOME

QUESTIONS ARISING OUT OF THE CONTROVERSY
RESPECTING THE PENTATEUCH.

London and Cambridge:
MACMILLAN AND CO.
1863.

ADVERTISEMENT.

THE opening Letter in this Volume was suggested by Bishop Colenso's work on the Pentateuch. But it touches on several points which have only an indirect connection with that work; it omits many which the Bishop would, no doubt, consider important. The Letters which follow are strictly in reply to the first, not the least a refutation or review of the book which called that letter forth. The final one states the impressions of the Layman respecting the answers which have been made to him.

CONTENTS.

	PAGE
LETTER OF A LAYMAN	1

LETTER I.
INTRODUCTORY 13

LETTER II.
IS REVELATION A WORD ONCE GIVEN? 19

LETTER III.
SUBJECT-MATTER OF THE BIBLE; HOW IT MUST BE READ 25

LETTER IV.
MORAL AND PHYSICAL STUDIES 33

LETTER V.
BIBLICAL APOLOGIES 46

LETTER VI.
LAWS.—GENERALIZATIONS.—THE CHRISTIAN FAITH . 56

LETTER VII.
THE FACTS OF BISHOP COLENSO 65

LETTER VIII.

FAITH IN CHRIST, AND THE AUTHORSHIP OF THE
PENTATEUCH 79

LETTER IX.

THE PENTATEUCH 92

LETTER X.

THE DELUGE 107

LETTER XI.

CURRENT PHRASES IN THIS CONTROVERSY 119

LETTER XII.

THE LAW COURTS.—THE PEOPLE OF GOD.—ETERNAL
PUNISHMENT 127

LETTER XIII.

OPINIONS OF BISHOPS ON THE FOUNDATION OF OUR
HOPES 138

LETTER OF A LAYMAN 156

CLAIMS OF THE BIBLE
AND OF SCIENCE.

March 9th, 1863.

MY DEAR MAURICE,

I do indeed wish you to speak in plain language about the Bible to English Laymen at the present time. I will tell you why, and I should be glad, as one of your oldest friends, though much severed from you through life, to tell others why.

For more than a quarter of a century you have been helping Englishmen to see through the theories and systems which have been invented to prop up, restore, develope, or narrow the ancient edifice of their National Church; and amidst ceaseless contumely and misrepresentation levelled against yourself, you have striven to teach, as Alexander Knox and S. T. Coleridge taught before you, that the Bible and the Church of England, in all their comprehensiveness, can best bear witness for their own truth, and for God's providence, against infidelity and Pantheism.

Now that many are shocked by Bishop Colenso's theories, or alarmed lest his criticism should put the faith of England in danger, I think you, who have been familiar with such questions all your life, can tell us how little there is to fear from a searching inquiry into facts. The only ground for alarm is lest a false and untenable position be taken up.

It is now thirty-five years and more since you migrated from Cambridge by way of London to Oxford. There are many now in high posts of responsibility who will remember that, bringing with you the inquiring and loving spirit of Julius Hare, and more experience of life than we had, you roused us to long for something deeper than logic, and helped us to look beyond that thin nominalism by which Whately and others were upsetting old notions without putting anything solid in their place. How Hampden's appeal from dogmas to facts was denounced as the *Foundation of the Faith assailed in Oxford*, and what advantage was taken of the reaction to build up the fabric of authority, we need not now discuss. Much earnest work has been done for which the English Church may be thankful. If we are humbled and made more indulgent to each other, by our several errors, mistakes, and failures, by the loss to our communion of some noble spirits, God's work may yet be acknowledged in what seems to awaken fear, and faith may be strengthened.

Meanwhile, whatever dreams, and notions, and schemes may have occupied the minds of men and women, the reality of physical, moral, and political facts has asserted itself. Laymen who have to work in the busy world, or in scientific investigation, are influenced accordingly. One feeling, however, is uppermost in the minds of those who are not absorbed in their own affairs; namely, the desire that the clergy should look facts in the face, as they hope to guide the consciences of their brethren by the light of principles.

During the years which have elapsed since we parted at Oxford, you have been at work with agricultural labourers near a large manufacturing town, with the sick and suffering in a large hospital, with medical students, with practising lawyers, and, for the last ten years, you have been specially engaged in reading the Bible and English History with the self-improving working men of the metropolis; you ought, therefore, to know something of the English laity—and many of them know enough of you to listen to what you have to say.

The laity are now appealed to from opposite quarters to stake their faith and their hopes of eternity on the results of arithmetic and criticism, and on the possibility of reconciling God's holy word in the outward form, in which he has been pleased to give it to us and our children, with the tangible facts of the world—that world of which "the Book" tells us that "all things were made by him" (the Word), "and without him was not anything made that was made."

How well I remember the place in which you first pointed out to me the connection of that truth with life and light!

Before I proceed to state the questions which I wish you to answer, let me, at the risk of repeating commonplaces, explain the position of parties as they appear to me in the case we have to deal with.

One of the most conscientious labourers in the field of science once indicated to me what he deemed the true relation between Science and Revelation.*

Science is essentially progressive, and therefore of necessity changeable, and in any given age imperfect. It is only the sciolist who lays down the law in practical matters, and says, "It has now been demonstrated beyond all possibility of doubt." The true philosopher says humbly, "In the present state of our knowledge it appears that such a law or fact has been ascertained." The more intense the attention given to one class of facts, the greater the necessity for not overlooking collateral considerations.

Revelation, on the contrary, is God's word once given. Our comprehension of that word may possibly be progressive, but it is necessarily imperfect, generally because all human knowledge is imperfect, specially because the subject-matter is different from that of ordinary knowledge, and because we are told that we must fulfil certain conditions, and use certain means, in order to attain to a knowledge of God.

Science and Revelation therefore are, so to

* See Note, p. 181.

speak, in different planes, and cannot come into real collision: unless we confound the one with the other.

Any man who feels this to be a true statement of the relation between Science and Revelation, may be excused if he takes no interest in the arguments of those who strive to prop up Revelation by remarkable confirmations founded on Science; or who struggle to protect the Bible from some imaginary danger, to be apprehended from the last new theory propounded at the British Association. Indeed, it is impossible not to feel some impatience when one hears those who know little of science, but wish to serve the cause of religion, attempt to show that the author of the first chapter of Genesis was inspired to use language which should, by a special miracle, anticipate and include all the changing phases of human discovery.

Those writers who so handle the truth, whether of God's word or of his world, are trying an experiment on the faith of the laity, tending to produce more serious results than all the doubts and difficulties which they seek to remove.

The reply of Dr. M'Caul to Mr. Goodwin in the 'Aids to Faith,' following, as it does, on

Hugh Miller's last work, seems to bring such attempts at reconciliation to a climax. It stands in remarkable contrast to the candour of Professor Browne's paper in the same volume, which admits and deals fairly with principles now working in the minds of many reflecting men. If it be true that physical science is leading its students gradually to an overpowering consciousness of a vast unity of plan in Nature, and of the continuity of general laws, it is the more necessary that the one living "God the Father, "Almighty Maker of heaven and earth," and "his only-begotten Son," "who for us men and "for our salvation came down from heaven, and "was incarnate," should be preached to sinners on grounds apart from physical laws; and that the "Holy Ghost," "who spake by the prophets," should be "worshipped as the Lord and giver of life" to us in this nineteenth century, whatever may be the results of human inquiry into the documents handed down to us as the outward form of God's holy word.

Doubtless many earnest-minded young men in the present day are perplexed, as we were in our younger days, by abstract questions, and metaphysical difficulties; but Bishop Colenso, avoiding all such questions, appeals to the test of what he calls facts. His conception of facts seems strange, and his deductions from doubtful data remind one of Coleridge's metaphor of the pyramid standing on its apex. I cannot presume to judge of the temper, motives, or spirit with which he has entered on his work, or of the results to which he may be driven if he pursues his present course.

My business here is only with the present influence on the lay mind of his alleged facts, well known as those facts (so far as they are facts) have long been to scholars, but entering little into ordinary clerical instruction, and hardly at all into current English literature, and therefore now for the first time to be appraised for what they are really worth by English piety and good sense.

The attempt to fasten on Bishop Colenso all the consequences of his hastily-drawn inferences, including a charge of moral dishonesty (however provoked by his unmeasured language, and however veiled under the form of a remonstrance), is, to say the least, in the present circumstances of the English Church, premature; nor is the attempt unlikely to increase the importance attached by the unlettered to false issues arising out of data of which he offers one solution, as if no other could be probable or possible.

But any one may venture to say so much as this: first, That it is contrary to all analogy to suppose that he has found at once the true solution of the difficulties he has elaborated. Secondly, That all his arithmetic and scholarship, whether they are torn to pieces or not, are secondary matters in comparison with the questions how we are to hear and receive God's word without equivocation, and how we are to rescue the Church from being proclaimed in a chronic state of siege, under attack from Science, or from placing itself in an attitude of hostility to critical inquiry properly conducted.

There are two questions to which a layman may naturally at the present time ask for an answer:—

1. Do not our faith in Christ, and our belief in the four Gospels as a real history, rest on grounds independent of the results of any critical inquiry into the authorship of the Pentateuch?

2. May we not continue to read the Pentateuch as the Word of God, speaking of man and

to man, without putting a forced construction on the plain meaning of the words, and without imposing fetters on the freedom of scientific or critical investigation in any matters which God has given us the power to inquire into?

With these two questions I should be disposed to close my letter, having purposely abstained from all metaphysical questions, and all theories about inspiration.

But I cannot help seeing, and therefore, in all honesty, I am bound to admit, that a third question, a most solemn and awful one, is oppressing the minds of those who love their Bibles, and who cling to the infallibility of the letter of Scripture as the ground of all their hopes.

I will not attempt to state the general question in distinct terms, but I may mention one illustration. Those of whom I speak seem to fear that if they once allow the historical reality of the physical account of the Deluge to be called in question, they are guilty of doubting the word of Him who is Truth. Thus faith in Christ is made contingent on the proof or disproof of the existence of certain natural phenomena. Or, to put the matter in another and perhaps more correct form, certain phenomena, which undoubtedly do exist, seem not to accord with the language of the Bible. Hypotheses are suggested (involving often a variety of supposititious miracles), not with a view to give a natural explanation of the facts, but to bring them within the letter of the Bible; thus, the belief in Christ's heavenly promises is apparently made to stand or fall with the probability or improbability of the hypotheses suggested.

It appears to me deplorable that such an issue as is here implied should have been raised. It is still more deplorable that it should have been countenanced, however unintentionally, by those in authority. You will best know how to disentangle the question from the mass of irrelevant matter with which it is encumbered. You will also be able to judge how far it is expedient that it should now be discussed.

I must leave you to consider how far the discussion of the Law of the Church on the "Sufficiency" or "Infallibility" of Holy Scripture, or of the consequences deduced from arbitrary definitions of the terms "Word of God" and "Inspiration," will help the solution of the questions I have proposed?

Living, as I do, in the country, I may be quite behindhand in my appreciation of what is going on in the minds of thoughtful men.

If the questions are not put clearly, the name of the querist will neither add to their relevancy, nor to the value of your reply; so I will only say that I am, with grateful recollections of the past, and hearty hopes that your future labours may bring comfort and blessing to yourself and others,

Your sincere friend,

A Layman.

LETTER I.

INTRODUCTORY.

My dear Friend,

The first impression which I received from your letter was one of mere delight at being remembered and recognized by an old friend. When I thought of it, there was much to qualify that impression. Shame and repentance for wasted opportunities and duties unfulfilled, was mingled with an uneasy suspicion that I ought to take part in a controversy which for many reasons I had avoided, and for which I had persuaded myself that I was incompetent.

Your enumeration of the advantages which I have enjoyed for acquaintance with various classes of the laity—with young men at both the Universities—with medical men—with lawyers—even for a short time with agricultural labourers, and now, in London, with mechanics, startled and shocked me more than you can well imagine. Our paths have, as you say, lain so widely apart almost since we were at Oxford together, that you cannot guess how very little I know of any of these classes. Partly a terrible shyness, partly a much less excusable indolence and cowardice, have kept me from understanding those among them who would not have refused me their confidence if I had sought it rightly; many who did seek it have been repelled by the coldness of my nature or my method of expressing myself, which has hindered them from understanding me. These faults have had much to do with the censures, which have been, you think in your kindness, too liberally bestowed on me. I have no business to say that they have been uncalled for. I know that when they have irritated me most they have been immeasurably less painful than the reproaches of my own conscience, which has told me how much better they were deserved than the praises of friends which have always overweighed them.

Still, whatever reasons I have for expecting a very small audience, I have published so many books that it would be affectation to allege any feeling of this kind as a motive for not plunging into the discussion which is now stirring so many minds. I had determined to abstain from it, because I supposed that a Hebrew lore, and a knowledge of science, which I do not possess, ought to be combined in every person who engaged in it; and because the Bishop, whose name has been introduced into it so frequently, is one from whom I have received much kindness, and who has stood by me when I have been attacked. To utter any words which might increase the odium under which he labours would be dishonourable to me; yet I could not express myself respecting his recent opinions without showing that I dissented from them as widely as many who have denounced both him and me vehemently.

Your call, however, is one which I must not disobey. You ask me for some words upon points which I have been considering seriously during many years, which all my circumstances and occupations have compelled me to consider. I shall not be obliged to affect any knowledge which I have not; possibly my very ignorance of physical science, and my partiality for studies of another kind, may make any testimony I can bear on its behalf of more worth; possibly my lack of the learning which would enable me to illustrate the Old Testament, may make what I may say of the good which, as one of the people, I have derived from it, less suspicious. If I have not the intimate acquaintance with the Laity for which you give me credit, I have at least mixed more with them than with the Clergy; they may think me freer from professional prejudices than some of my brethren. The question, as to the merits and demerits of Bishop Colenso, has reached a stage which will enable me to speak of him without appearing to court the favour of his accusers; I hope, without inflicting any fresh wound upon him. But most of all, it is your allusion to old times, and to the hopes which you once formed of me, that forbids me to be silent. The first theological book, now long out of print and forgotten, which I wrote, has a value in my eyes for the intercourse with you into which it led me. We both thought then that the Articles of the Church had a much closer connection with the University and its studies than with the Catholic Church; that the Creeds were the bond of union to the people; that the Articles were useful to those who were seeking a learned culture, and were needing to be warned against some errors and superstitions which might interfere with it. We have both, I doubt not, altered our opinions about the wisdom of calling laymen to subscribe a formulary which they evidently do not receive in this sense, which they look upon as a mere bondage upon their consciences. We may both begin to doubt whether the subscription of clergymen is not becoming a snare to them also. But I have been confirmed by an experience of thirty years in the general principles, which I maintained in that pamphlet. I still think the articles were not intended as terms of communion. I am still grateful to them for the service they have rendered me in warning me against different partial opinions which I might have accepted from different schools, in warning me against my own private opinions, in pointing me to a truth which embraces all our narrow conceptions of it.

Many of the friends whom we cared for most, and who took most interest in these questions, are gone to their rest. Those who remain are probably too busy in public affairs to remember mere academical disputes. But a new generation has arisen, to which we are bound by many ties as closely as to our own. If anything I should write in answering your letter can save them from any of the mistakes into which we fell; can point them a way out of their own special temptations; can turn the fathers more to the children, and the children to the fathers, you will not be sorry that the events of a recent time have recalled one that has gone by.

I will waste no more time in preface. I propose to consider the different paragraphs of your letter in succession. I am far too apt to follow a method of my own. I am most thankful that you have marked out one for me.

Ever yours affectionately,

F. D. MAURICE.

LETTER II.

IS REVELATION A WORD ONCE GIVEN?

My dear Friend,

Your friend's distinction between Revelation and Science is accepted very generally by men such as you describe him to be, and by divines. To dispute it is an act of boldness. Yet I must commit that act, for I am persuaded that nearly all the difficulties which beset us most at this moment,—nearly all those awkward attempts at reconciliation of which you complain with so much reason,—have arisen from the open or implicit adoption of the doctrine that Science is progressive, while Revelation is " God's word once given."

Supposing the etymology of the word Revelation were in the slightest degree the key to its signification, it *cannot* be " a word once given." It must denote an unveiling or discovery. And if it is, as we are wont to say, a Revelation of GOD, the unveiling must be a gradual one, adapted to the capacities of the creature to whom it is made. We should assume that Revelation had this force if we were not told the contrary. Of course, we may be told the contrary. A Mahometan is bound to hold that the Revelation which he thinks is contained in the Koran is *not* of this kind. That is for him " a word once given." It comes in after our Scriptures, confirming a part of them, annulling a part, giving what it adopts the same stationary character with itself. I beg you calmly to examine every passage in which the word ἀποκάλυψις occurs in the New Testament, and to ask yourself whether in *any one* that word can bear the Mahometan sense; whether in each one it must not have the sense which I said we should naturally give it if we had heard of no other. I will go over the instances, one by one, if you wish it; but I would rather that you trusted *Schmidt's Concordance*, and your own observation of the context, than me. I would rather you tried to find one instance from which you could infer directly, or by a process of reasoning, that Revelation is not the Discovery or Unveiling of that which has been hidden; I will add, any considerable number of instances in which it does not import the discovery of a divine Person.

But I am aware that the mere examination of the uses and applications of the word, however steadily and carefully pursued, will not be satisfactory. Such an examination cannot, of itself, conquer an impression so widely diffused,—for many reasons so natural to us,—as that to which the Mahometans generally, and so many Christians, laymen and divines, have yielded. Leave the phrase then, and turn to the course of the Bible narrative. Whether that narrative is *historical*, as opposed to *fabulous*, is a question belonging to another part of the subject. I am now speaking of the *form* of the book, not of its credibility. That form is obviously historical. No book that you ever read contains so few formal propositions. All of it is connected with persons and with life. The laws and decrees are imbedded in what assumes to be,—whether it is or is not,—a record of the growth of a people. The idea which is expressed in the 11th chapter of the Epistle to the Hebrews, that the fathers were always expecting some better thing than they had, so that they *without us could not be made perfect,* is the idea of the Bible throughout. Must there not then be some great fallacy lurking in the notion that Revelation differs from Science because it is not progressive? Is not progress an essential characteristic of it, if we assume the Bible representation of it to be the right one? Has it not been so esteemed by the most orthodox students? Is not "a progressive unfolding of the Divine purpose" one of the stock phrases of theologians?

But are you quite confident in the correctness — or at least the completeness — of the other branch of the statement? Is the idea of *discovery* strange to the mind of the scientific man? Is not discovery what he is always looking for, always aiming at? But discovery imports the removing a cover from something that *was* while it was hidden, that is not changed by becoming known. Science is not progressive *in this sense,* — that it makes anything be which was not. It rejoices to disclaim any such faculty. It boasts of *finding* fixed, permanent, universal laws. I do not ask the scientific man to say that GOD discovers to him any law or principle. To many that might not be real or honest language, — or they might not feel it to be so, — therefore they should not adopt it. To many, I doubt not, it is the most simple, genuine expression of their inmost thoughts. But, at all events, *I* am bound so to speak. Believing the Bible to be true, I cannot suppose that any discovery can be made to a man except by God. I must suppose that when at last it bursts upon him it is a gift from God. I must suppose that all the previous processes of inquiry which have led to it; the circumstances which have assisted it or appeared to hinder it; the blunders, the disappointments which have been the instruments of humbling the intellect of the inquirer, and delivering him from rash conclusions; the hopes, and the fears that nourish hope; have all been foreseen and overseen. I repeat it, with the Bible in my hands, I cannot interpret the struggles of the scientific man in any other way than this. Whilst, therefore, a " word once given " seems to me a very inaccurate description of a divine Revelation, in so far as it denies that to be a gradual unveiling and unfolding of Truth, I can imagine a sense of that phrase which a student of physical science would not consider inapplicable to his experience. He too asks, and receives; he seeks, and finds; he knocks, and it is opened to him. The " word " which he speaks to his fellow-men has first been " given " to him.

Ever yours affectionately,

F. D. MAURICE.

LETTER III.

SUBJECT-MATTER OF THE BIBLE; HOW IT MUST BE READ.

My dear Friend,

You go on, after defining Revelation to be *God's word* once given, "Our knowledge of that word may possibly be progressive, but it is necessarily imperfect, *generally* because all human knowledge is imperfect, *specially* because the subject-matter is different from that of ordinary knowledge, and because we are told we must fulfil certain conditions, and use certain means, to attain to a knowledge of God."

You will observe that I do not identify the progressiveness of Revelation with the progressiveness of our knowledge. Following the lessons of all great theologians, those lessons which we must heed if we speak of the Bible as a history, or distinguish between the Old and New Testament, I have spoken of God's unveiling of Himself as gradual. I have accepted the doctrine that God spoke in sundry times and diverse manners, in preference to the notion of "a word once given." How this language of the Epistle to the Hebrews is compatible with St. Jude's respecting a "faith once delivered to the saints;" nay, how impossible it is to accept that faith in its fulness whilst we borrow our notion of the Bible from the Koran, I shall endeavour to show hereafter. I ask no more now than that you should not assume your definition of Revelation to be the Bible definition of it.

But if the Revelation has been progressive, the knowledge which has answered to the Revelation *must*—not *may*—have been progressive. The eye can receive no more light than is vouchsafed to it. The eye may be closed against that, but just so far as it is opened, it takes in just what is presented to it. Is not this true in the physical world as well as in the moral world? Can you establish any distinction between them on this ground?

But there is a distinction, you suppose, from the imperfection of the knowledge in the one case. You do not mean this. You confess that the imperfection applies in *both* cases. Our knowledge of God is very imperfect. Our knowledge of the world, you will be the first to admit, is very imperfect. You complain of divines for wishing to hinder the removal of some of the imperfections under which it labours. But while you allow a *general* imperfection in all human knowledge, you maintain there is a *special* imperfection, arising from two causes, in the case of that knowledge about which the Bible is conversant. It arises from the subject-matter of that knowledge. It arises from the conditions which are demanded for arriving at that knowledge.

Each of these points deserves a careful consideration. What is the subject-matter of that knowledge with which the Bible is conversant? You would say, perhaps, that it is the supernatural, the transcendent. But see! There is no book which speaks so much of shepherds and their flocks, of the most ordinary doings of families, of nations and laws, and wars; of all that we are wont to call vulgar and secular things. You might call the subject-matter of the greater part of the Book of Genesis, the disputes between brothers, and the famines which afflicted Palestine and Egypt; the subject-matter of the Book of Exodus, the escape of certain tribes from captivity, and their wanderings through a desert; the subject-matter of Leviticus, the management of sacrifices, and the treatment of diseases; the subject-matter of all the books of the Old Testament, the various fortunes of an Eastern people. And only by the most violent and tortuous processes can you separate what may be called the transcendent or supernatural part of the narrative from these affairs of common life.

Must we not then say that the Revelation or unveiling of the divine or supernatural, if it is made at all, is made *through* these relations of ordinary daily life? Is not this the great characteristic of the Book, the one which, if we take it to be the record of a continuous Revelation, prepares us for the full manifestation in the Son of Man? Now this is, no doubt, a different subject-matter from that of the physical philosopher. One has to do with *human* life: with *things*, the growth and decay of things, with the Cosmos of things, only as they are related to man, only as they speak to man. The other is occupied mainly with the growth and decay of things, mineral, vegetable, animal; with man as connected with these things; with man as part of this Cosmos. The difference is the same essentially as that between the subject-matter of the studies in the school of Anaxagoras and of those in the school of Socrates. The latter we are wont to speak of as *more* closely connected with the earth than the former. Socrates boasted that they were so. The question was then, and is now, whether the road to the highest heaven is through the stars or through man. But Socrates never affirmed that the inquiries of Anaxagoras were false because his own were true. If he was ever tempted to adopt that conclusion, it will have been because he distrusted the *method* of his former teacher, because he regarded him as a speculator rather than as one who investigated facts. The teachers of the Bible in our day have not *that* pretence for discrediting the studies which are prosecuted in the schools of physical science. They know that the method there is tentative and experimental; that facts are reverenced above all speculations. Woe to them if they find *any* excuse for treating facts, or the laws which lie beneath facts, lightly. If they do, they will treat the Bible lightly. They will misunderstand its scope and method.

They will lose their faith in God Himself. With religious phrases on their lips, they will become Atheists.

And this brings me to your remarks about the conditions which are required for arriving at the knowledge of divine truth. Surely they are stern conditions! It is a straight and narrow way which leadeth to life! There must be a continual waiting for light; a distrust of our own assumptions; a readiness to be detected in error, certain that God's meaning is infinitely larger than ours, and that other men may perceive an aspect of it which we do not perceive; a belief that He is fulfilling His promise "that all shall be taught of Him," in ways which we cannot imagine; a dread of shutting out any truth by our impatient notion that it must contradict some other; a determination to maintain what little has been given us in the hope of its expansion, and never to contradict, if we understand ever so little, what may have been given to another; a resolution to hold the ground on which we stand, without judging him if he cannot yet see what this ground is. Hard is it to form these habits of mind; I covet them more than I can express, and believe in my sane moments that the Spirit would educate us all into them if we would but submit. Yet I fall continually into habits the very opposite of these. And I cannot help perceiving that this mind, the mind of the little child, the mind which our Lord demands of us, has been exhibited by many scientific men who have been censured and scorned by the religious world of their day, and has been sadly deficient in their accusers. All would confess now that Kepler was right in his belief about the constitution of the world, and that those who condemned him for appearing to contradict Scripture were wrong. I cannot be content with saying this. I cannot read those beautiful extracts which Canon Stanley has made from Kepler's defence of himself without hearing a testimony in my inmost conscience: 'That man was trusting in 'God. He had been converted to be a little 'child. Those who were trampling on him were 'not acting as servants of Christ, but were full 'of the intellectual pride, the arrogance of spirit, 'which Christ condemns.' I dare not judge them. If I had lived in their day, I should probably have added my weak voice to swell the shouts of those who had the upper hand. But I think I could not have abided the searching eye of Him who said, "Judge not according to appearance, but judge righteous judgment." I think He would say to me, "Knowest thou not "the truth which I demand in the inward parts is "not tested by the favour of men? Knowest thou "not that priests and rulers pronounced Me a "blasphemer?"

Affectionately yours,

F. D. Maurice.

LETTER IV.

MORAL AND PHYSICAL STUDIES.

My dear Friend,

"Science and Revelation," you say, "are therefore, so to speak, in different planes, "and cannot come into collision unless we con-"found the one with the other."

So far as the "therefore" in this sentence refers to the assumption of a difference between Science and Revelation, because the one is progressive, and the other improgressive; because one concerns the things of earth, and the other the things of heaven; because the habits of mind and the moral discipline required for them are dissimilar;—I must, in conformity with what I have said in my first two letters, dissent from your conclusion. But I have intimated that there is a ground upon which I can accede to it, provided the terms of it are a little altered.

The student of the Bible and the student of physics are, I conceive, moving in different planes *in this sense*,—that any discoveries which are made to the former must be through the relations and conditions of human life; that the whole order of the universe must be for him subordinate to man, and contemplated in reference to man; that for the other, human life is only one of the facts of the universe; its order must be regarded as comprehending man. The forgetfulness of this distinction between the functions of the moral and the physical inquirer has been a fruitful cause of "collisions" between them in all ages. They have occurred, and would occur continually were there no Bible, and were no transcendent worth attached to its teachings. The collisions ought, I conceive, to be fewer, at last ought to cease altogether, *because* such a book as the Bible exists; *because* we accept it as marking the true order and character of the discoveries respecting man. If it has not produced that effect, if the Bible has been made an excuse for the collisions, this must be owing, it strikes me, to some of those mistakes, respecting the object and form of the Bible, at which I hinted in my first letter; to some of those transgressions of its commands, departures from its spirit, neglect of its warnings, upon which I dwelt at the end of my second letter. Scientific men may have been guilty of these, more or less. But I am not able to estimate *their* mistakes or *their* temptations, whereas I do know something of ours. And if we profess to be teachers of the Bible, we must be bound to a clearer understanding of its purpose, to a stricter observation of its maxims, than they can be.

You think " that a man may be excused if he " takes no interest in the arguments of those who " try to prop up Revelation by remarkable con- " firmations founded on Science." I entirely acquiesce in this opinion, though I do not accept your statement of the relations " between Science and Revelation " as a true one. I feel it difficult to " excuse " any believer in the Bible who *does* look out for these remarkable confirmations. I cannot help suspecting him of feeling a little insecurity about the ground upon which he is standing. He is paying a compliment to physical science, which, though I reverence it greatly, I cannot pay it. He is tacitly asserting that physical demonstrations are more trustworthy than moral demonstrations. I do not confess them to be so; and I believe that much of our fearfulness about the Bible results from a secret notion that they are so. I cannot help seeing, however, a good as well as a bad side in this eagerness for physical confirmations of moral truths. There is latent in it, an acknowledgment that the results of the two methods must ultimately harmonize if each is pursued faithfully. The mischief lies in the feverish anxiety to get this result at once, and in the sacrifice of fidelity to which such anxiety inevitably leads. The religious world offers a premium to the scientific inquirer to make his conclusions fit the Bible conclusions. So it produces a race of quacks, who can always prove what they are wanted to prove; men in spirit much like the false prophets of old. And it often, I am afraid, bribes men of real insight and diligence to suppress or misrepresent facts and their own convictions, lest they should injure their reputation. A heavy price is paid for these momentary triumphs. The discomfiture which follows of course, appears to shake the edifice which had been buttressed so feebly and so needlessly; numbers suppose that the very foundation of it is undermined. And yet this is the smallest part of the calamity. To obtain these physical facts on its side, the Bible suffers greater perversion and contraction than the facts have suffered. We lose the very messages which it delivers to us, whilst we are straining our ears for proofs that it is not deceiving us.

That "struggle to protect the Bible from the "last new theory propounded at the British As- "sociation," which you so justly despise, is another effect of this passion for "confirmations." If we can get any distinguished member of the British Association to speak in our favour, we are full of ignominious rapture; if any of its members throw out opinions which contradict ours, or may lead to a contradiction of ours, we are full of a terror as ignominious. I know no more encouraging proof that the God of truth is still among us, much as we are offending Him with our lies in His Name, than that the faith of scientific men in the Bible has not wholly perished, when they see how small ours is, and by what tricks we are sustaining it. "I have listened," said an old official of a certain University, "for forty years to the sermons at St.——'s, "and, thank God! I am a Christian still." Thank God! there are Christians still among scientific men, though they have been listening for more years than those to our defences of Christianity.

You go on, "It is impossible not to feel some "impatience, when one hears those who know "little of science, but wish to serve the cause of "religion, attempt to show that the author of the "first chapter of Genesis was inspired to use lan-"guage which should by a special miracle anticipate "all the changing phases of human discovery."

I dare say you have heard many speak thus who know little of science. Hear then one who knows almost nothing of science, and who, though he thinks that the cause of religion does not want his support, yet, being called to teach the Scriptures, has been led to meditate somewhat on the first chapter of Genesis, and who loves it the more he meditates upon it.

If I supposed that it anticipated all the after revelations of God which the Bible sets forth to us, I could not believe the Bible. St. Paul speaks of *a Revelation of things which had been kept secret from the foundation of the world, but now are made known to His holy Apostles and Prophets by the Spirit.* If I supposed that it anticipated the discoveries which God has made to physical inquirers, respecting that order and constitution of the universe with which physical inquirers are occupied, I must not only reject the Bible generally, but I must reject this portion of it particularly. For I cannot read this document without perceiving that the words, "God made man in His image," are the words upon which the meaning of it all turns. Treat those words as an interpolation, refuse to look upon them as cardinal words—and the whole of the chapter, as the unfolding of a divine order, is emptied of signification. But so long as these words are retained, and are regarded as cardinal words, we must treat the order, which the Bible contemplates, as a different order from that which the physical student contemplates. The elements of which it consists are the same; there are in both earth and sun and stars, plants and trees, birds, beasts, fishes, Man; but these are looked at in an altogether different relation to each other. They compose, I can use no other expression, a different Cosmos. Whether it is possible that the same subjects should be looked at under these two different aspects, whether there can be an order in which Man is regarded as the Bible regards him—this is a question which I do not require the physical student to decide hastily. The history of past ages,—the experience of the present age,—tells me that it is an exceedingly difficult one for him to pronounce upon; that he has many motives which must incline him to suppose the Cosmos, which has been discovered to him, the only one. I am equally persuaded, by the evidence of past history, and by the experience of this time, that he will not be able to rest in this conclusion; that a thousand arguments, wholly apart from any influence which the Bible or the religious opinions of the day may have over him, will drive him out of it; that affection for his family, interest in the doings of his own nation, and of all nations, hints flashing forth from his own studies when they appear most to tend in the opposite direction, will bring him to claim a position for himself and his race which they cannot hold — which they have no right to hold — in his cosmology. I have the profoundest confidence in God's lessons coming through these experiences. I have the least possible confidence in our reasonings.

My business, however, is not chiefly with the men of science, but with men of my own profession; men ignorant as I am of science, or blessed with some apprehensions of it. They *must* accept both these modes of contemplating the universe; they cannot preach God's Gospel to men except they fully and heartily recognize the one; they cannot sail in a ship, or travel by a railroad, without confessing the other. Many things, indeed, in the management of a ship, in the construction of a railroad, may suggest to them thoughts of human dominion which will accord well with the lesson of the first chapter of Genesis. But they must be aware that relations between the heavenly bodies and the earth are presumed in navigation—that there are facts of hydrostatics and dynamics presumed in the existence of steam-power, and the use of it—which are not taken account of in this chapter, and *could* not be taken account of it, if it were true to its own purpose. If this be so, then it must be a solemn duty for the divine—in justice to his own calling, that he may not abandon the truth of which he is the guardian—*not* to attempt an adjustment of two statements different in kind, which never can be adjusted except at the sacrifice of the simplicity and integrity of one or both.

But after the numerous efforts at adjustment, which were made when geology first began to be studied, and have been made recently, such a maxim as this will be more easily proclaimed than acted upon. The return to simplicity, like the return of a frozen limb to warmth, is full of suffering. The man who is aiming at simplicity will often seem to be more artificial than his neighbours; he will be conscious how little he attains his aim. I feel as much as you can do the difficulty of not connecting the words, " Let there be light, Let there be a firmament," with notions of a material manufacture. And yet I am sure, when I read all such passages as these which represent the very mind of the Hebrews, *By the word of the Lord were the heavens made, and the earth by the breath of His mouth*, that no such notions as these—that the very reverse of these—were conveyed to them by their divine oracles; that *they* belong to an artificial manufacturing age; that I cannot disengage myself from them, because I am living in such an age. Such a temper of mind did not belong to the shepherd boy, to whom the heavens declared the glory of God, and to whom the firmament showed His handiwork, to whom day after day uttered speech, and night after night taught knowledge. I may not be able to place myself in his point of view; to look at the world as he looked at it. If I could, the first day would tell me of God calling forth the light; the second, of His giving a fixed order to sky and earth, land and water; the third, of His evoking the productive powers of earth; the fourth, of His bidding the sun and stars appear; the fifth, of His awakening to life all the creatures of the deep; the sixth, of His bidding the animals live, and of His making man in His own image; the seventh, of the divine rest, and His delight in what is very good, in the unity of His works. Following that course, it would never occur to this shepherd boy to think of the world as consisting of huge continents, islands, and peninsulas. The little spot on which his home stood would receive the light each morning, would be spanned by a firmament, would contain its garden ground with grass and herbs, would be shined upon by sun and stars, would not be far from some river full of fishes, would nourish its own cattle, would have its family of human beings. He would never be obliged to journey back over centuries and millenniums, or to task his fancy with the question what might have been when these things were not. They were there, and God, at the beginning, had said that they should be there. Thus every day creation would seem to him very old and very young. His belief,— God spake, and it was done; He commanded, and all things stood fast,—would not interfere with the feeling "Each day He maketh all things new." Every day he would think that he glorified the God of Abraham by discovering, so far as his means permitted, fresh treasures, which He had hidden that His creatures might search them out. That it was in this way the noblest Hebrews looked at the creation, I gather from the Psalmists and the Prophets. That their minds were open to receive fresh light from fresh circumstances, I learn from those wonderful visions of God which were granted to Ezekiel, as he lay beside the river of Chebar, when the forms of Babylonian sculpture were presented to his outward eye. But the recollection that their God, the God of their fathers, created the heavens and the earth, kept them from the worship of things in heaven and earth; kept them from the dread which makes the investigation of these things impossible. Whenever we Christians have lost this Hebrew culture, we have sunk into an idolatry that has denounced science as wicked and dangerous. May not the mixture of that idolatry in our minds now have far more to do with our fear of physical inquiries and speculations than our reverence for the first chapter of Genesis?

Affectionately yours,

F. D. Maurice.

LETTER V.

BIBLICAL APOLOGIES.

My dear Friend,

You say, in reference to some who suppose that the first chapter of Genesis anticipates the discoveries of physical inquirers, " The writers " who so handle the truth, whether of God's Word " or of His world, are trying an experiment on " the faith of the laity, tending to produce more " serious results than all the doubts and difficulties " which they seek to remove."

Such a warning from an earnest layman ought indeed to make a clergyman pause and ask himself what mischief he is or may be working, whilst he thinks he is doing God service. Looking at the subject from my own side, considering how these experiments have injured the Book which they profess to defend, I cannot doubt that you are right. The first chapter of Genesis, read as it is written, is full of wonder and simple beauty. The message which it has brought to generations of men, and may bring to generations more, is not merely obliterated, but contradicted, by those who would use it either to support or to control the conclusions of the physical student.

I do, nevertheless, most fully and firmly believe that so far as it has been left to tell its own tale,—so far as it has made itself heard above our noisy interpretations,—so far its influence has been immeasurably more quickening and beneficial to physical studies than those who engage in them know. Sir Charles Lyell, if I do not mistake, speaks of the valuable hints which the geologist finds scattered about the Hindu cosmogonies. Of such hints so laborious and honest a student as he is would of course avail himself. He might, for a time, be fascinated by finding through what cycles of ages, so unlike the poor seven days, the imagination of those world-framers had travelled. But after paying all the respect which is due to such dreams,—and men who find that there is a waking reality corresponding to them cannot withhold such respect,—what has been the actual result to those who have grown up under this vast heap of thoughts about the universe? The learned Brahmin has to implore the help of the West,—fed, as it has been, upon the Bible,—to extricate him from his systems; not that he may become a Christian, but that he may look any fact of science in the face, that he may dare to confess it. The Englishman or German can actually take possession of his books, and find a sense in them which he, with all his marvellous acuteness, is by himself unable to find. For the Englishman and German, whether he has kept the conviction or not, has grown up in the belief of a Creator of heaven and earth. The world is not his god; he has not to find his gods in the world; therefore he can examine it freely; he has been told that God hides His counsels that man may search them out; therefore search is for him a duty.

Nor can I overlook this consideration. You will not bring us to tolerate some of the startling observations which are made by physical students on the relation of our race to the lower creatures, as well as on the processes of destruction which are going on among those creatures (and among men so far as they are of the same kith and kin with them), unless you have something to balance these observations, unless you can point to some relation which we have to a higher nature, unless you can assert a law of life, beside the law of mutual destruction. Sir C. Lyell quotes a saying of Mr. Hallam, that if man is made in the image of God, he is also made in the image of an ape. Be it so; let the physiologist detect the relationship to the ape in any way he can, in any way facts warrant him in doing it. Only let us have some right to tell him of his other kinsmanship; only let us be able to assure him that he can have a divine eternal life, and so rise above the tendencies to death and to murder which are in him. Then the more courageously that other region is explored, the more reason have we to be thankful. Let the physical inquirer make out the affinity of each of us to the ape—such humiliation is seasonable and profitable; but he shall not hinder us from bearing witness to him, that *he* has a glorious parentage; that *he* has the nature which was redeemed by the Son of God. I do not say that he will believe us when we say this, or that he is bound to believe us. I only say that whilst we profess a reverence for the Bible,—whilst we call it a Book of Life, a Book concerning the Image of God, and the discovery of that image to man —*we* are bound to take this course. And one reward for taking it, as I think, will be this: We shall sustain all the observations and experiments of the man of science; we shall correct anything which may be one-sided and narrow in his conclusions, without throwing the least obstacle in the way of his arriving at such conclusions, or complaining at all of them for being one-sided. If we are right, his conclusions ought to be so; and are the more correct, as drawn exclusively from the premises with which he deals, because they are so.

You will see, then, that I cannot relish more than you do, any 'Aids to Faith' which interfere with these inquiries, or try to prohibit them as inconsistent with the Bible; I should name such interferences 'Hindrances to Faith.' Whether the particular essay of Dr. M'Caul's, to which you allude, has this character, I am unable to decide, not having read a line of it I should be grieved to see an excellent man, for whom I have a high respect, employing his great learning, which ought be turned to such account for the Church, in the work of exposing other men's errors, if that work were performed ever so ably.

If I thought my faith would be stronger for undergoing that pain, I should submit to it cheerfully. But I am afraid, from some experience in these controversial writings, that even the best of them might operate the other way; so I have abstained—except in the case of one essay which contained reflections upon some valued friends of mine—from looking into the volume of which you speak. I can, however, imagine,—in my ignorance it is better to make a favourable than an unfavourable conjecture,—that a writer so strongly Hebraic in all his feelings as Dr. M'Caul, may have been as much offended as I was—contemplating the question from my English point of view—by Mr. Goodwin's notion that the writer of the first chapter of Genesis was an early 'Descartes.' There is something to me curiously infelicitous in this conception. It involves as huge a moral anachronism as I should think ever suggested itself to an ingenious and scientific man. And yet it is one which deserved a careful treatment, seeing that by the quiet examination of it we might hope to banish for ever the notion, not unsanctioned by some divines, that what we have been wont to call the Mosaic record of Creation, is in any sense whatever, an attempt to imagine or form a world. Descartes has told us so very clearly, in his own exquisite language, how he proceeded in his work of construction—he did that work in so masterly a manner—that there cannot be a better *experimentum crucis* than the one which he affords of the difference in kind between him, the seventeenth-century philosopher, and a man—call him Moses, or by another name—who looked out upon the objects, which every peasant in any corner of the earth must behold, and who, in simple, authoritative, brief words, tells the peasant, 'Your God, your 'Deliverer created this; and this, and this. See 'how the cattle feed and bring forth. He bade 'them feed and bring forth. See how the sun 'rises like as a bridegroom out of his chamber. 'He bade it rise at the beginning, and still 'bids it rise now.' I trust that Dr. M'Caul,— of course with the kindness which he always exhibits when not engaged in controversy, and which is eminently due to a man so thoughtful and serious as Mr. Goodwin—has pointed out the absurdity of this and all similar comparisons, and has set an example of discarding for ever the attempt to spoil the truthfulness of the Hebrew records by mingling them with the results of inquiries pursued in a method and for an object altogether different from theirs. Such a service to the cause of which he is the able champion, was especially demanded of him; if he has rendered it, I cannot understand how he can have committed those outrages upon scientific freedom of which you complain. I am afraid, therefore, that, in his eagerness to overthrow an adversary, he must have forgotten what was due to his own cause, and must have supplied one more example of the wounds which the Bible has received in the house of its friends. I should have supposed that Dr. M'Caul's dread of German idealism would have led him to welcome with peculiar satisfaction that zeal for fact, and patience in investigating it, which are the great counteractions of this idealism, and which appear nowhere so remarkably as in our scientific men.

If Hugh Miller was ever faithless to facts and investigation, he must indeed have lost the use of his right hand. I should judge, from the only book of his which I am competent to speak of, 'My Schools and Schoolmasters,' that he was the best witness left in Scotland against the taste for abstractions by which his countrymen are so much infected. But if, in any weak moment, the national passion got the better of him, he may have been more helplessly immersed in the quagmire, because he had never before walked except on firm ground.

In conclusion, then, I plead guilty for myself and my order to the substance of the charge which you bring against us. I must take, however, what I think is not a frivolous or captious exception to the form of it. I do not think we have made too great a demand on the faith of the Laity. I fear we have not appealed enough to the faith of the Laity. If we had invited them to faith in God; showing that *we* had faith in Him; that *we* could trust Him to vindicate His own purposes; if we had acknowledged that He, who spake by Apostles and Prophets, is indeed speaking in every insect and flower,—there would have been a response to our call, and perhaps in no class of the Laity more than in the scientific men. We have spoken, not to their faith, but to their fondness for controversy and disputation. We have tried to prove how cleverly we could use all weapons, some of them weapons which are fetched straight from the devil's armoury. If in such a battle we should be defeated, if when we ride on horses those who pursue us should be swifter, we, not our faith, must bear the blame.

Affectionately yours,

F. D. Maurice.

LETTER VI.

LAWS.—GENERALIZATIONS.—THE CHRISTIAN FAITH.

My dear Friend,

You say that "Physical Science is "leading its students to an overpowering con-"sciousness of a vast unity of plan, and of the "continuity of general laws." Blessed of God must Physical Science be, if that is its tendency! Such an overpowering consciousness is what we especially need to deliver us from our frivolity; to make us ashamed of our rhetoric; to bring us low before the Lord of heaven and earth. And we have Scriptural warrant for the belief that the contemplation of physical facts does lead to this overpowering consciousness, and to this humiliation. There is only one cardinal passage (if we except the rapturous 104th Psalm, and those at the end of the book) upon the subject, but that, to a believer in the Bible, is decisive. Job, wearied with his own speculations and the speculations of his friends about the cause of suffering and moral evil, at last hears God Himself speaking out of the whirlwind. A glimpse —a little glimpse—is given him of a vast unity of plan; of laws affecting the least and greatest of the creatures which surround him. The consciousness which follows is described as indeed overwhelming. The result of it is that he says: "I have heard of Thee by the hearing of the ear, but now mine eye seeth Thee. Wherefore I humble myself, and repent in dust and ashes." I do not doubt that it may be the purpose of God to speak in like manner to this generation. Woe to us if we try to hinder His voice from reaching it by the loud discords of ours!

But you feel that those of us who have no vocation to deal with physical facts, who only prove ourselves bunglers and darkeners of counsel whenever we meddle with them, have yet a duty to mankind,—a duty made more imperative upon us by the vigour and earnestness of the students of nature, and by the great effects which they are producing. You have indicated our obligations most accurately, and you have thrown out an important hint respecting the help which we may give to men of science, still in promoting—not checking—the freedom of their investigation, whilst we faithfully fulfil the trust that is committed to us.

The student of physical science, and the student of theology, have, I believe, a common enemy. We have talked so much of these things in former days, that I shall not startle you as I should many Oxford men, by saying that I mean the generalizations of the logician. I hope I am not insensible to the worth of logic, or unthankful to the new light which has been thrown on many parts of it since the days when we studied it, especially by Mr. Mill and Sir William Hamilton. I have learnt something, and might have learned much more, from these eminent men; but I cannot conceal my opinion that Mill's 'Essay on Liberty' is a very remarkable protest against some of the perils to which his own logical completeness is exposing us; or that Sir William Hamilton's testimony against our attempts to see things as they are in themselves, is a testimony against the imperfection of his own instrument, and a confession that we need some other, if Science is not to be a dream and an impossibility. Each of these teachers seems to assert—is understood by his disciples to assert—that we cannot look through or beyond appearances; that all which we dignify with the name of laws are only our generalizations from appearances. Each, I think, having a high purpose, is hampered by this determination of his intellect, and often, in practice, breaks through it; yet each, from his very honesty and logical consistency, stoutly maintains that it must not and cannot be broken through, and suspects every one of transcendental leanings—even if he be a hard mathematician—who speaks otherwise. In Mr. Mill's case this tendency is strengthened by the habit, acquired in the school of Hobbes and Bentham and not overcome by his broader and freer culture, of treating the use of the word Law as merely metaphorical, when it is not applied to human creatures, and when it is not connected with some formal penalty.

Now, I cannot think that that "overpowering consciousness," of which you speak, will be produced in any man of science who bows before what he feels all the while to be a generalization of his own understanding. I cannot persuade myself that Mr. Faraday, or Mr. Owen, or Mr.

Darwin, or Mr. Huxley, though they may all express themselves in conformity with the scholastic usage of their day, fancies that he is only practising a feat of ventriloquism; that he only hears echoes in Nature of his own voice; that he only finds what he has first hidden. I am sure he has a simpler and grander faith than this; that he often starts, 'like a guilty thing surprised,' at the apparition of a truth or principle which, after long seeking, bursts upon him; that he is sure it was *in* the facts, and that it now stands before him, the *Law* of these facts; something laid down of old, though it may first be made known now. And I think that we who, through direction of our studies, happen to know a little of the tyranny of the logician in other spheres, and what rebellions that tyranny has provoked, should put the man of science on his guard, and encourage him to hold his own stoutly. The writer of the 'Novum Organum' did so much for us divines in throwing down the idols which the logicians had set up, that we are bound, as far as we can, to return the service in kind. The idols are rising again under new names; we have the most intense interest in breaking them into pieces, and grinding them small. If we can do that, we may protect the physical student from assaults which may ultimately render all his investigations abortive, though, in his devotion to those investigations, he may be indifferent and secure.

Generalizations substituted for eternal laws and principles—these I regard as the plagues and curses of the theologian and of the physical student equally. I told you that I did *not* acknowledge Revelation as a 'word once given,' and that I *did* acknowledge a Faith once given to the Saints. I did not acknowledge the one, because I acknowledge the other. It seems to me that the Bible records the gradual revelation—the divine evolution—of that Name into which we are baptized; that Name about which you ask, with such striking and pathetic earnestness, whether we cannot still believe in it, "whatever "may be the results of human inquiry into the "documents handed down to us as the outward "form of God's holy Word."

My answer is this: If by that divine Name we understand certain generalizations of ours concerning it, certain intellectual conclusions which have either been transmitted to us, or at which we have arrived; those generalizations will be subject to all the accidents to which our intellects are subject; they will be various as our intellects are various. They must depend at first upon our confidence in the authority or judgment of certain men who have imparted them to us; next, upon our conclusions respecting the balance of arguments in favour of or against their being legitimately deduced from the Scriptures; then, upon our opinions respecting the probability that all those Scriptures can be ascertained to be of divine authority; ultimately, upon our opinions respecting the nature of divine authority. And, oh! what a question that last is! A *divine* authority which must rest upon the deference which we pay to a *human* authority, or to the sagacity and security of our own judgments respecting that human authority! Finally, we must enforce these conclusions of human authority, or our own judgments about it, by prohibitions and persecutions; for the sake of whom? Of the ignorant multitude—of the women and little children—whom we have actually cut off by our conditions from the possibility of knowing the truths which we are so tenderly preserving for them!

Can this monstrous and hideous contradiction last? No! for God *is*. And it is written in the Bible that He wills all men to come to the knowledge of the truth and live. Suppose we actually hold those words to be divine; suppose, we think further—it is not too great a supposition for Churchmen of the English Church or any other—that we *are* baptized into the Name of the Father, the Son, and the Holy Ghost; and that the faith in that Name is the faith delivered to the Saints which we are to cherish, and for which we ought to die; must we not say—can we help saying—that our faith is in divine persons, not in our generalizations; faith in a Being whose thoughts we cannot measure or compass, but in whom we live, and move, and are; faith in Him who has promised to guide us into all truth; faith in Him of whom we may know a little here, whom by slow degrees, in ages out of ages, we may learn to know. If there is such a Name, if we are sealed with it, can our apprehensions of it depend upon the judgments which any have formed in any day about texts of Scripture, or about the human authority which pronounces on texts of Scripture, or about the documents which contain texts of Scripture? All questions on this subject may be interesting and important in a very high degree; but if the Scripture sets forth a Revelation, and if the Revelation has issued in this wonderful discovery, must we not suppose that GOD, as the Bible says, *has founded* His Church, *and that the poor of His people may trust in it?* Can we desire anything for that Church but the fullest, freest search into principles and laws? For God must preside over that search; it must lead to the exposure of our ignorance; it must issue in the manifestation of that Love, the height, and length, and depth, and breadth of which St. Paul desired for us all that we might know, even while he said that it passed knowledge.

Affectionately yours,

F. D. MAURICE.

LETTER VII.

THE FACTS OF BISHOP COLENSO.

My dear Friend,

You say in one clause of your letter: "Whatever dreams, and notions, and schemes "may have occupied the minds of men and wo- "men, the reality of physical, moral, and politi- "cal facts has asserted itself. Laymen, who have "to work in the busy world or in scientific in- "vestigation, are influenced accordingly." There cannot be a better introduction to the remarks which I have to make respecting the Bishop of Natal. Of him you observe that, avoiding all metaphysical questions, "he appeals to what he "calls the test of facts."

Assuredly that is his claim. The impression which he has produced in England is derived from this cause. He has excited the fears of those Englishmen who wish to believe the Bible true, because he is supposed to have disputed its message, not on metaphysical grounds, but as at variance with facts. He has excited the hopes of those who wish to believe the Bible false for the same reason. His opponents try to prove that he is mistaken in his statements, that he is feeble in his scholarship, in order to dislodge him from this position. By no other test than that which he has himself chosen, can he—so all confess—be fairly tried. I grant you also that Laymen are the persons to apply this test. *We* have various prejudices. *We* shall be apt to mix religious or metaphysical considerations with the pure naked facts. Let the Laity, those men who are busy with the affairs of the world—those of them, if you like, who are engaged in scientific investigations—be the jurors. There should be a fair mixture of the two classes. Let the scientific men be there, only not let them exclude the busy men.

For, as you observe so truly, there are certain moral and political facts which are asserting themselves, as well as physical facts. Neither must be overlooked. The physical facts are worthy of all consideration; but if those who are specially interested in these boast that they are the *only* facts—if everything which belongs to the human region, which has to do with the acts and sufferings of men, is treated as fantastical and not real—we must, not as clergymen at all, but as plain Englishmen, in the interest of the Laity, and their common business, speak up stoutly, and declare, 'This shall not be. Numbers 'are good. Weights and measures are good. All 'honour to them. But man must have *his* honour. 'His transactions may not be capable of being 'brought under the rules of arithmetic or geo-'metry, but they are *bonâ fide* transactions not-'withstanding. The world in which we dwell 'cannot dispense with them.'

Now I must repeat to you remarks which I have made elsewhere, and which are far from being to our credit as clergymen; that the Bible is not in any sense our book; that we did our best to keep it from the Laity; that we fed them as long as they would suffer us with legends, pictures, and mere dogmas; that after awhile they would not bear this; that they said they would have the Bible, and have it in their own native tongue; that they claimed it especially, emphatically, as a *history*—in contrast to the legends, or the mere school opinions which we had doled out to them; that they craved more particularly *in this sense* for the portion of the Bible which Bishop Colenso now declares to be not historical; that they used this portion of it against us and our pretensions, saying that it bore witness of One who was above all priests, who called them, and kings also, to account for their evil doings, who governed the world Himself, and did not trust it to our mercies.

These are facts with which every reader of English history, and of the history of any nation of Christendom that cares for the Bible, and has adopted it into its common life, is perfectly familiar. And I wish you to observe how truly this lay movement, this rebellion against the Clergy, was an acknowledgment of " facts which had as-" serted themselves." They were not physical facts, not facts of arithmetic. They were political facts, which had for them the " sternest " reality." They were called to be citizens, fathers, husbands, brothers. How could they be actually what they were meant to be? How could they claim their rights; how could they understand and fulfil their duties? The Clergy had not taught them these rights and duties. They had been encouraged to bring their gifts to the treasury of the temple, and so to be free of obligations to fathers and mothers. They had been told that to renounce civic life was a virtue. If there was a Lord God who had proclaimed His commands out of heaven amidst thunders and lightnings; if He was really what He said that He was, a Lord God who brought His people out of the house of bondage; if He had indeed redeemed slaves in Egypt out of the hands of a tyrant; if He had plagued the tyrant, and thrown his hosts into the sea; if He had led the poor captives through that sea; if He had fed them with manna; if He had struck the rock for them; if He had borne with their murmurings, and complained of them for not trusting Him always and in all places; if He was the same from generation to generation; if the laws which men confessed to be binding upon them, were still laws that went out of His mouth; if He cared for the freedom and order of nations now as of old; if He was jealous over them now as of old, not willing that they should throw themselves into the hands of enemies and oppressors; if He punished them now as of old, that He might deliver them from the ruin they had brought on themselves, and do them good at the latter end; if this were so, then England might live, then Englishmen might hold up their heads against their foes, and rise up where they were ever so sunken, in the might of Him who had promised not to forsake them, or to forget them; not to turn away His mercies from them, but to pardon the transgressions of them, their kings, their prophets, and their priests, and to love them freely.

I know what idle sounds these are in the ears of many of us, what mere repetitions of old Hebrew phrases. But people conversant with the 'stern reality of political facts' did not find them so, and do not find them so at this day. To them, the dead phrases are words of life and power—trumpet cries awaking them out of their sleep, bidding them cast off the slough of their cowardice—such as they can hear from no modern preachers of liberty, from no "party of action." They raised the English middle classes into moral and political existence; they ratified the great oath of the Swiss peasants at Rütli; they raised the Dominican Savonarola to be the witness against Alexander VI.; they made the German monk mightier than Charles V.; their echoes woke again among the peasants of the Tyrol;

they stirred the scholars of Germany to a new life; they roused the Czar of the Russias to drive back the invader who had profaned the holy shrines of Moscow. When the 'sternness of 'political facts' has no more asserted itself; when the ease and luxury which spring from civilization and destroy it have taken place of toil, and zeal, and hope; then this Old Testament phraseology has become flat indeed; then it has been left to schoolmen and rhetoricians; only the hearts of a few women have borne witness that it has a voice for the personal and domestic, as well as for the national life; only the Laity have felt as the people of Cologne felt about their Cathedral, that the very scaffolding has a sacredness. They have a respect for the shell of the words, if the life has gone out of them.

But this respect for the shell, if it endures among the easy and respectable middle classes of our land, will not endure—I am sure of that— among the working classes, especially in times when bread is scarce. Words must either live for them, or they will be treated as carcases which are to be buried. Can we say to them: " The God who rules over you is verily such an " *one* as this book—taken in its simplest sense—

"says that He is. We proclaim to you that "God is the Deliverer of captives. He did not "pretend that He delivered them; He actually "delivered them?" I believe that we may do this; I believe that it is our sin—the sin of us Clergy—that we have not done this. I believe we have shown our distrust in the letter of the book which we profess to regard as divine, by not doing it. I believe that we are all involved in this sin, and that God will call us all to account for it, and will torment us and our land for it. I believe we have represented Him as an altogether different Being from Him whom the Pentateuch sets before us; and that He is calling us, in manifold ways, to repent of our slanders against Him, and to speak of Him to the people as the Bible speaks.

Now, just as some of us were beginning to feel these things,—I do not say earnestly or thoroughly, but so much that we could not be quite easy in making the brass sound and the cymbals tinkle,—just as the 'political facts' of England's condition were becoming rather too 'stern' for us—we heard a loud 'Eureka' from a distant colony. A Bishop came over to us, and spoke to this effect: 'I have ascertained by the clearest evidence that all this story, to which your fathers turned from the legends of the friars, and the dogmas of the schools, is itself a mere legend. You, Laymen, are not bound to believe it. Churchmen, you must not preach it any more. I went out, thinking I could tell it to the Zulus. They did not understand it at all; they have led me to examine it. I find that the statements about numbers in it are incompatible with physical facts which I must acknowledge. Therefore, while I admit that it may contain some useful spiritual lessons; whilst I do not impute any worse motives to the compilers than those which may have been at work in Homer, or any other poet, I say distinctly this is not history.'

This is that appeal to the test of facts which you speak of. As such, it has been recognized and accepted by some of the scientific Laymen, by no small portion of the Clergy. As such, it will probably be accepted by no small portion of the working classes. As such, it has been vehemently denounced. Its propounder has been decried and scorned. The answers to him, so far as they have not consisted of shrieks and ridicule, have been directed to an exposure of his physical facts. *They*, it is said, are not what he says they are, or, if they are, it is better not to take notice of them, because they may disturb our faith. The Bishops, who have addressed him, *appear* to say: 'Your opinions about these physical facts interfere with your position in the Church. Therefore we request you—though we may not be able to command you—to leave us.' That is the interpretation put upon their words by the Laity. Whether it is the correct one or not, I do not venture to affirm.

Now, I apprehend that if the physical facts on which the Bishop dwells, are as he alleges they are, no possible arguments of ours can shake them, or diminish their validity. And if they are so, that they should be known and confessed, must be right. We are dealing falsely with God, we are not believing in the God of Truth whom the Bible sets forth, if we wish to hide them. But now supposing them admitted, what then? Is the Bishop's inference that the *history* of the Book perishes—that it must be disbelieved—if we do justice to these stern physical facts, a reasonable or a tenable one? The more you examine it, the more unreasonable and untenable, I think, it will appear; unreasonable and untenable, I mean, if the Bishop's own fact-test be applied to it. Numerical facts are valuable, important, indisputable. But they do not constitute history; they do not even constitute the evidence of history. A very great exaggeration in numbers about the Expedition of Xerxes —if it can be proved—may make me doubt the information, or even the veracity, of Herodotus. It will not make me doubt the truth of a battle of Salamis and a battle of Platæa. It will not make me doubt the grand truth that a set of tiny European republics discomfited the great monarchy of Asia. These events are taken out of the region of letters. They do not depend any longer on the credibility of records. They have established themselves in the very existence of humanity. You cannot displace them without destroying that, or remaking it anew, according to some theory and fashion of your own. Yet how little did it signify to the Middle Ages, occupied though they were with great and living questions of their own, that there had been a Salamis or a Platæa! Such facts are seized when they are wanted. The narrative of them then becomes intelligible, becomes credible. They remain credible and intelligible so long as the need of them is felt. You cannot produce faith or understanding by criticism. You cannot shake faith or understanding by criticism. But you may by criticism or without it make men doubt and reject that which they have ceased to understand as connected with themselves, as interpreting their own lives.

I think no one felt more indignation than I did against Bishop Colenso. He seemed to me to be taking from us the very message which we had been suppressing and mutilating; to be indorsing the crime which we had committed against the Laity; to be using physical facts for the sake of cheating us of moral and political facts; to be destroying the great link between God and national life; to be driving us to the old platitudes and abstractions about the necessity of order to freedom, and freedom to order, which have no power over any human spirit, when we might, if we believe the Exodus, speak of an Everlasting God of Freedom, who is also, and for that reason, the God of Order. He was robbing us of the *facts* of God's Revelation, and so throwing us upon religious ideas, the 'God consciousness,' and all that talk which means something to Germans, but to an Englishman is the substitute for a meaning.

But the more I have watched the history of this controversy, the more I have perceived that my wrath cannot work out the Righteousness of God; that I have been unjust to the honesty of a man struggling with great difficulties in his own mind; that I have not estimated the greatness of our offences, or the degree to which his offences are chargeable upon us; that, above all, I have not confessed how God is leading us by strange ways back to the faith which has departed from us. We have worshipped the letter of the Bible till we are unable to read the letter of it. The Exodus does not tell *us* of the God whom it proclaims; it does not tell *us* that He is the Lord our God. We talk of it and its authority, and its infallibility. HE is not in all our thoughts. We do not trust Him, but a theory of our own about the correctness of a document. In all ages God has broken these confidences in pieces. It was this confidence, in the Pharisees, which led them to destroy the express words of the fifth command; to invert the meaning of the fourth; to tell our Lord Christ that He broke the law, and that He was a blasphemer. If the Bishop of Natal and his arithmetic are instruments in overthrowing this idolatry, they may be instruments in making the history which he tramples upon, once more real and precious in our eyes. That he should not discover the worth of that history whilst he was following the tradition of Protestant missionaries in translating a book into a barbarous tongue for a barbarous people, which only gave out its sense to Europeans when they had felt the stirrings of a national life, and had a language capable of expressing more than animal wants,—need cause us no wonder. The preface to his book shows us that he has retained his faith in a God, 'whose everlasting arms are under us.' If he commits himself to that God, I doubt not he will be delivered from his conceits and denials. If we commit ourselves to the same God, we shall be delivered from ours.

Affectionately yours,
F. D. MAURICE.

LETTER VIII.

FAITH IN CHRIST, AND THE AUTHORSHIP OF THE PENTATEUCH.

My dear Friend,

I come now to your questions. The first is this: "Do not our faith in Christ, and our "belief in the four Gospels as real history, rest "on grounds independent of the results of any "critical inquiry into the authorship of the Pen- "tateuch?"

That I may answer this question with the seriousness and directness which you would desire, let me remind you what I, as an English clergyman,—sent to preach of Christ to my countrymen, accepting the Bible and the Creeds as my guides how I should preach of Him—must mean by faith in Christ; what I must suppose the four Gospels, if they are a history, to set forth. You will then see, I think, how far it is possible for me, without renouncing my calling and my orders, to make our faith in Christ dependent upon an opinion respecting the authorship of the Pentateuch.

I am certainly not using peculiar language, unorthodox language, when I say that I am bound by my office to speak of Christ to men of this day as their Prophet, their Priest, and their King. I must tell them that He died for our sins, and rose again for our justification. I must tell them that He speaks to us now as He did to our fathers; that He is our Mediator at the right hand of God; that He rules over our spirits, and souls, and bodies, over the families and nations of men. I must say that He is the Eternal Son of God, begotten before all worlds, the Light of Light, the very God of very God. I must say that He took our nature to claim us as sons of God in Him. I must say that He came to baptize us with the Spirit, and so to give us power to be sons of God.

All this it belongs to my function as a clergyman of the English Church to declare to people of every class; because I have confessed it to be true for people of every class, a truth which God has wished His creatures to know, and which He has demonstrated to their consciences, notwithstanding its strangeness and improbability, and their reluctance to take it in.

Other men, of course, may consider this message as an idle tale. But you are writing to me, knowing what I have professed. This, then, is what I try to preach about Christ. This is what I think the Church bids me preach concerning Him. And therefore, when I take my subject from the four Gospels, I say: 'Here you have
'a discovery of what He is, to whom you are
' closely related, of whose body you are members,
' who is fighting against your enemies, who is
' working in you by His Spirit. Here I find
' how He manifested His power over men, and
' His sympathy with them, during the years
' that He dwelt upon earth. Here I learn the
' nature of that Kingdom under which you and
' I are living, and how all outward and visible
' things explain and illustrate it. These Gospels
' answer to their name, because they carry me
' beyond themselves. They point me to a Person,
' a Word in whom is Life, and whose life is the
' Light of men. They commend you and me to
' His guidance. If we submit ourselves to it,
' we shall know more of these Gospels, of our

'selves, and of each other, than I, and all the 'preachers in the world, can tell you.'

Now, supposing we did speak thus in sincerity and truth, would it not be almost an insult to ask us: 'Does your faith in Christ depend on your 'belief in the authorship of the Pentateuch? 'Do you wish other men's faith in Christ 'to depend on their belief in the authorship 'of the Pentateuch'? And if any one had put this question to an Apostle, to a true missionary of any age or school,—to Boniface, to Xavier, to Schwartz, to Henry Martyn,—I think it would have been an insult, though such men were not likely to resent that, or any other which was offered them. I think it would have been an insult to any Reformer, to any Evangelical preacher of the last age. Belief in Christ had for all these so profound a signification; their sense of the necessity of Christ to all men was so mighty; they were so sure that it is the Father who draws men to Christ, and not arguments or arrays of evidence; that they could scarcely have brought the terms of your proposition home to their minds. But to *us* it is no insult at all. The Laity have the greatest right to press such demands upon us. We are bound to face them.

Oh, if they might lead us to examine our ways, and to ask ourselves solemnly in the sight of God, *what* we have been believing, *what* we have been teaching which can afford an excuse for the opinion that we require an exercise of judgment upon a certain document before we can allow men to trust in their King and Saviour!

We must be perfectly aware that nineteen out of twenty of those to whom we proclaim the Gospel,—to whom we must proclaim it, unless we exclude those from it whom the Pharisees wished our Lord to exclude, *the people who knew not the law, and are cursed,*—have no capacity whatever for examining the authority of documents, or for pronouncing any judgment respecting the writer of them. 'But if they do not 'hear any disputes about them, they will take the 'author on trust, they will yield to the common 'opinion.' Perhaps so; and will their trust in that common opinion have anything whatever to do with faith in Christ? Will it advance them one step towards faith in Christ? But they *do* hear disputes about these things; they *will* hear disputes about these things. How then? Are we not to bid them to believe in Christ? are we not to preach His Gospel till we have settled their minds on this point? How shall we settle them? By arguing about it, and then insisting, under heavy denunciations, that they shall come to but one conclusion as the result of the argument? By resolving that Moses *shall* be proved to be the author of the Pentateuch, and declaring that our proofs must be accepted? And this, while we are saying the book is God's book, and not the book of a man at all; that the book is to be received on His authority, and is not dependent on human reasonings! In what a weary circle are we moving! How are we setting aside faith in the very act of insisting upon faith! How are we indorsing and canonizing rationalism—the determination of our own intellects—in the very act of declaring it to be devilish!

If I entered into an examination of the steps by which we have been brought into these terrible contradictions, I should have to go through much more of our ecclesiastical history than you would have leisure to consider. It is better to inquire with all earnestness how we may be extricated from them. It seems to me that God is Himself extricating us from them, if we only confess His hand in the affairs of churches and of men, as we, at least, are bound to do. Can we really reverence Him and His government, if we suppose all these questions of criticism, all these arguments respecting ,the books which are most sacred in our eyes, have been stirred without His knowledge or design? Do we hold that the eye which never slumbers or sleeps has been indifferent to these movements in the minds of His creatures? Is it not very strange, what Leighton would have called " very brutish," for Christian men to cherish such an opinion as this? But if there is some purpose in the direction which the minds of some men in this age have been taking towards these critical inquiries—if we, who do not feel much call to engage in them, who do not experience that strong compulsion of the age, which the Bishop of Natal tells us that he cannot resist—ought we not to inquire, ' Is there no message coming out of them for us? Is God teaching us nothing by them?'

If we do not stop our ears, I think He will teach us very great, if they be very humbling, lessons by them. I think He will lead us *back* to the faith of our fathers, *onwards* to the apprehension of a truth which they could not fully receive, which was darkened by some of the conceits of their own minds. I join these two hopes together; for me they are inseparable. Many think there is a great progress to be looked for. But we must obtain it by renouncing the most cherished convictions of the old time. Many think that we must by all means recover the faith which we have lost, or which is departing from us; that we must recover it by consenting to abandon all thought of a larger knowledge, a clearer spiritual light, than that which was vouchsafed to the sixteenth or the seventeenth or the eighteenth century. If this is so, we are in exactly the opposite position to the students of physics; for the condition of progress with them is the recognition of the light that has been granted; and, on the other hand, the torch must be dimmer than it was in the last hand which held it, if it is not fed with fresh oil, if it does not bring forth something that had been hidden. But we are still more unlike the Prophets of the Jewish Church, who always rebuked their countrymen for falling away from their trust in the God of their fathers, because they were thus shutting their eyes to the higher blessings which were reserved for their descendants. If this is so, we are separated from the good men of every time, who have comforted themselves in all dejection respecting their own age, by recollecting the things which God had done in the times gone by, and by expecting a Revelation of the Son of Man which should fill the whole earth.

First, then, if it be true, as all in some way or other admit, that our fathers did believe in Christ directly, as an actual Person related to them; if it be true that such a faith as this, and not one grounded upon evidence respecting documents, must be the faith of women and little children; are we not solemnly warned that our attempt to make criticism give out one answer or another is not more dishonest, according to its laws, than it is injurious to the very cause with which we suppose criticism is interfering? You prove Moses to your satisfaction to be the author of the Pentateuch. Be it so. Now go on. What next? You will argue from the Pentateuch that Jesus Christ is the Son of God, the Saviour of the World. Perhaps you may: and perhaps, if I believe in Christ already, and have confessed Him to be my Lord, I may see some force in your arguments, —or rather, I may see some force in the words about which you are arguing, and which you are exceedingly likely to overlay and kill with your arguments. But to ascend from the Pentateuch to Christ; to prove that because that is, He must be; who taught you this method? Is it the Apostolic one? Is it one which commends itself to any man's conscience in the sight of God? Is it not utterly dishonourable to Him whom you profess to serve? Is it not this which God in His good providence is confounding and making ridiculous, on purpose to show us that men do need a Christ, a Son of Man; that they are crying for Him, wailing after Him; and that we have no right to hide Him from them, or to impose any hard intellectual conditions, any preliminaries of ours, to the admission of Him as the Everlasting Word, as the Deliverer, and Teacher, and Judge of the Universe?

But, secondly. If I thus bring myself into harmony with the good and wise of other generations, from whom I have gone astray in the vain ambition of displaying my intellectual prowess and discomfiting some conclusions which I account dangerous,—I may also discover what it was that hindered those wise and good men from always trusting their own Gospel, from always committing it to God,—as in their sanest and devoutest moments they did,—to take care of it, and to bring all men to the knowledge of it. They knew in their hearts that it was not the testimony of men, but the testimony of God, which had brought them out of their narrowness and selfishness to trust in One who had given Himself for them all. They said so again and again. And whenever they spoke what they meant in prayers and thanksgivings, it was this same testimony they recognized as the source of all faith in their fellows; it was this testimony they desired for those who were in darkness, who did not see the thing as it is. But there crept over them, as there does creep over all of us, the notion that this testimony of God concerned *them*, and not their race; that *they* were to know Christ truly; that the majority of men could only know Him in some secondary sense—in what they said, in their exhortations and warnings, was no sense at all for any moral or spiritual purpose. Yet they could not quite give up their conviction, taught them so continually in the Bible, that the Gospel was for all sinners, for the whole world. So they began, slowly and reluctantly, to admit a kind of outside religion for the use of people in general, resting not on the testimony of God, but of men. People born in

Christian countries must be taught generally that the Bible was the production of inspired men; that it had a divine authority; that its books were written by the men whose names they bear. Then a few who had gone so far might be admitted into the *arcana* of Christian faith, those *arcana* being what St. Paul said was the good news which he was to deliver to all nations.

My dear Friend! I must and will speak my mind. This is an accursed and a godless scheme, and I bless and praise God that the Laity are rising up to say that they will not endure it any longer. They must be drilled into a certain set of notions about books, that they may be prepared to receive that which is an eternal fact, or nothing! They must accept certain conclusions about human testimony, that they may be prepared to receive God's testimony concerning Himself! I rejoice that we cannot make out our points! I rejoice that people declare the evidence we produce to be altogether insufficient! I see another mind in all this than the mind of human scepticism and self-will. I see Him at work, who desires that all men, from the lowest even to the greatest, should hear the Gospel of the Son of God, and should live; who will not suffer us to cheat mankind of that Gospel, who will not allow us to withhold the doctrine that Christ is the Head of every man, the first-born of every creature. Our fathers did limit the message of His salvation, though they believed in Him with all their hearts for themselves, and for those who accepted Him. To regain the old ground, we are forced to conquer new.

I have answered your question exactly as it is put, adhering to the very letter of it. I have not inquired at all who is the author, or who are the authors, of the Pentateuch. Anything which concerns this subject will fall better into a consideration of the next topic you have raised. I thank you for the method you have followed in proposing these questions. It will seem to some not the chronological order. It is the right order. It is *for us* the chronological order. We profess to believe in Christ. That is our standing-point. From that we should start. The past may be very precious to us,—will be far more precious than it has ever been. But we shall not know its preciousness if we forsake what we have, and deduce our rights from it.

Affectionately yours,
F. D. Maurice.

LETTER IX.

THE PENTATEUCH.

My dear Friend,

Your second question is this: "May we not continue to read the Pentateuch as the Word of God, speaking of man and to man, without putting a forced construction on the plain meaning of words, and without imposing fetters on the freedom of scientific or critical investigation in any matters which God has given us the power to inquire into?"

After the remarks which I made in the last two letters, you will not wonder if I should answer: "I doubt whether we *are* reading the Pentateuch as the Word of God, speaking of man and to man." I think we shall *begin* to regard it in that light when we cease to put forced constructions on the plain meaning of words, and when we resolve to impose no fetters on the freedom of critical or scientific investigation in any matter. Such is certainly my conviction. I will try to show how I have been brought to it.

I cannot open the Bible in any part of it,—in the books of the Law, in the Psalms, in the Prophets,—without meeting with this expression: 'the word of God,' or 'the word of the Lord.' It is the characteristic expression in all these books, that which binds them to each other. The prevalence and persistency of this language is what any person, reading these documents for the first time, would feel to be their distinction from all others which he had ever met with. He would find, as I have said already, all Creation attributed to this 'word of the Lord.' That by it the heavens were made, is the familiar, the uniform phraseology of the Hebrew writers. But the falling of the snow, the coming of the frost in its regular seasons, or at any unexpected season, is equally traced to this 'word.'

The application of this language to natural things, often as it occurs, does not, however, exhibit the full import of it. You have described it with accuracy and fidelity to Scripture usage, as 'speaking of man and to man.' Whilst other nations thought of great powers which ruled in the sun or stars, which exercised dominion over man, to which man owed homage, and which he must propitiate, the Jew was taught always to think of a Being who addressed *him* directly, who had raised *him* above the works of His hands, who had given *him* dominion over sheep and oxen and all the beasts of the field. That superiority is especially indicated in the gift of speech. Man's power is through words. And words are the signs to him that he is made in the likeness of God, that he is intended for converse with God.

There is nothing which is so much to be desired as that "no forced construction" should be put upon "the plain meaning" of this phraseology. If we are to speak of the Bible as the word of God, we must let it tell us about the word of God. We cannot contract and subvert its own teaching, and then say that we accept it as the guide and judge of our acts and thoughts. And this, it seems to me, is what we have been doing. Just that sense of the word of God which is most distinctly set forth in the Scripture, which has commended itself to men's consciences as its most natural sense, which can be shown to have had most influence on the mind of Christendom—to have moulded its language, its literature, its arts, and have been most welcomed by the devoutest people in all ages, when their devotion was strongest,—just this is dying out of our minds, is practically rejected by the religious world. The belief of God actually speaking to men, of His speaking to men in all generations, of its being the greatest misery for any period not to hear His voice in the movements of the universe, in the transactions of kingdoms,—this belief, which alone makes it possible for us to attach any significance to His acts of old in Egypt or Palestine, which alone causes the existence of a Bible to be conceivable,—this belief is assailed and undermined—by whom? By those who are demanding the most unquestioning and unreserved assent to the letter of the Bible, who say that no errors can exist in that letter; yes, who say,—for this is the practical corollary to the former proposition—that *our* construction of the letter, *our* opinions respecting it, must determine what men shall think about any questions which may be raised either by students of human history or students of nature. What is meant, what is often said, is that the letter of the Bible *is* the word of God, that there is no other. It is admitted, perhaps, that there is a technical, artificial, figurative meaning of that word in which it was applied by St. John to our Lord Jesus Christ; but this meaning has nothing to do with the common one. *That* refers to the book only, and to the letters of the book.

Now, not in the least in the interest of physical science or of free inquiry—the champions of both would repudiate me, and probably call me very disagreeable names,—but simply as one who has learnt all he knows from the Bible, simply as a minister of the Word, I do solemnly abjure this doctrine, and protest against it. I am convinced that any Jewish prophet would have considered it as broadly and directly atheistical. I am convinced that any Pharisee, who hated Christ, would have given his unfeigned assent and consent to it, and would have made it,—why do I say would have made it, *did* make it — into the most powerful and cruel of his weapons against Him. And therefore the Pharisees could not understand what the prophets said of a Word of God coming to them, of a Word of God speaking in them, and speaking to the people. Therefore they could not understand how they should rebuke their countrymen for their deadness in listening to that Word, when He was addressing them, as He addressed their fathers, by sore trials, punishments, and daily blessings. And therefore *we* cannot understand those prophets. We must turn their message into figures, or nail it down to some event that happened once, or project it into the far future. As a message from Him, who is, and was, and is to come; as a message concerning *our* hypocrisies, our idolatries, it is nothing. To serve a political purpose indeed, to crush an opponent whom we cannot meet on a fair field, we do resort to Isaiah and Jeremiah, as if they had a great significance; we find them denouncing the Maynooth grant, and threatening those who vote for it. But our worship of gold, and our worship of the letter of books,—the prophets have nothing to say against these. They give no warning about turning to men whose breath is in their nostrils, and not heeding the Lord of Hosts. They do not tell us that He may be arising to shake terribly the walls which we have built, and which we are daubing with our untempered mortar.

I am speaking of the Old Testament generally. You wish me to speak of what we call the Five

Books of Moses particularly. We call them by that name. One of the first points which suggests itself to some persons in the consideration of them is, 'Have we a right to call them by that name?' I suppose, before we examine that point, there can be no objection to our reading them. On every hypothesis they must be worth something more than any notions of ours about them. Well, then, is the assertion of their proceeding from Moses, the most prominent assertion in them? Is that the one to which they especially demand my assent? Where do I find it? In Genesis? No! there the creation of all visible things is ascribed to the Lord God. There the government and punishment of men, and their restoration, is ascribed to the Lord God. There the Lord God is reported as calling Abraham, and bidding him go into a land which he shall be told of. There the Lord God is reported as speaking to Abraham, Isaac, Jacob, Joseph, and giving them wisdom; as speaking also to Abimelech and Pharaoh. But so far, at least, I have heard nothing of Moses, nothing therefore of his being the author of that book. I go on to Exodus. There undoubtedly I hear much of Moses. He is drawn out of the water. He grows up as a son of Pharaoh's daughter. He feels for his people. He takes a wild way of redressing their wrongs. He is an exile in the land of Midian for forty years. There GOD speaks to him. The name of the I AM is proclaimed to him. He is sent to tell the people that the Lord God of their fathers has seen their afflictions, and has heard their cry, and is come to deliver them. Moses, we are told, slowly and reluctantly yields to the divine call, submits to be the messenger of God to his countrymen. He has all opposition to encounter from them as from the Egyptians. But He who has sent him prevails over the tyrant; bears with the murmurs of the slaves, who long for the flesh-pots they have lost; educates them to trust through their distrust; orders their society; gives them laws, statutes, a tabernacle, and priests to minister in it. The Word of the Lord speaks to Moses assuredly. The Exodus may be called in all simplicity a Book of Moses. But, if we believe what it says, how can we care much whether Moses, or any one else, wrote down the letters of it? Is it different with Leviticus, with Numbers, with Deuteronomy, except that this last book contains the record of the death of Moses? Are not all discoveries to us of a divine Lord, speaking to man, and of man? Is not the interest, the beauty of the narrative, that the men who appear in it feel themselves to be witnesses and servants of Him; that they are just as ready to exhibit their own weaknesses, failures, unbeliefs, as any of those qualities which show that they had the divine image? Yet we must, in spite of themselves, without the slightest warrant and encouragement from them, call *them* infallible, so putting them between us and the divine Lord whom they lived and died to proclaim to us. And, as if that were not enough, we must exalt the letter of the book above these holy, inspired, but imperfect servants of the great King. We must make *that* more sacred than their living acts, more sacred than what they declared to be the triumphs and deliverances of the Living God!

Now, since all the attempts to impose fetters on the freedom of scientific or critical investigation arise from the notion that the letter of the Bible ought not to be subjected to the same kind of handling as the letter of other books; that disputes about the authorship of the books in the Bible are more dangerous than disputes about the authorship of other books; I might at once say, 'Such attempts are unlawful, because they 'are insulting to the majesty of the Word of 'God, because they suppose either that the Word 'of God is not really speaking to men in all 'ages, as the Bible affirms; or else that the 'Bible is the one book in the world which God 'does not care about, which is not safe under 'His protection, which we must patronize and 'watch over, and keep from injuries.' Priests and doctors in all ages have held this last opinion. They have looked upon the Bible as a feeble, tender plant, which was committed to their nursing, which they were not to let the winds of heaven visit too roughly. And the great proof of its vitality is, that it has lasted through all this nursing; that *they* have not been able to kill it; that their forcing-rooms and hothouses have been thrown down by the winds which they dreaded for it; that it has thriven, and put forth fresh leaves and richer fruits in the open air.

I would not, however, confine myself to generalities. The evidences of these facts are about us. This very controversy has brought forth numbers of them. The religious world complain of Bishop Colenso. What has he done? He has accepted their own dogmas. He has identified the letter of the book with the Word of God. He has not been able to read its own testimony respecting that Word of God. He has assumed that it is giving, not a revelation of God's ways to men, of His mode of governing men and holding intercourse with them, but a narrative of events which are unlike all other events that have happened in any generation since. Therefore he demands—reasonably demands—that there should be a minute accuracy in all the details of these events to ensure *their* credibility, which would not be needed to ensure the credibility of any other events. And the moment he misses that minute accuracy the whole vanishes into air. All that have appeared to mankind the most substantial facts, the great deliverances from fables, the great witnesses for a true God who is fighting with the false conceptions of men, become legends in his eyes; they may be as honest as the Homeric legends: he hopes they are; much more they cannot be.

It is easy to exclaim against such language. I am as ready to exclaim as any one, if I saw any good in exclamations, and if I did not fear that I might be denouncing a fair and logical deduction from premises which he and his accusers have equally accepted as sound. Is it not better to look into those premises than to quarrel with the conclusion? Or if the conclusion startles us, is not that a solemn call and obligation to inquire whether we may not be cleaving to a principle which involves it? If we are, surely we can only avoid the result by shutting our eyes; and we may not be able, any more than Bishop Colenso, always to keep them shut.

Still, is there not a fear of dislodging some old and dear faith whilst we draw this distinction, even though the Bible warrants it? Shall not we outrage the decisions of the Church even if we adhere to the doctrine of the book which the Church recognizes? There is an illustration, also taken from the present controversy, of that danger. The Bishop of Natal does not like to read the passage in our service about the Israelites being led through the Red Sea,—"figuring thereby thy holy Baptism." Of course he does not—of course he cannot. He feels Baptism to be a witness of a truth. He supposes the passage of the Red Sea to be a miraculous legend. But now observe how the composers of the Baptismal Service felt about this passage of the Red Sea, and how exactly, how felicitously, they expressed the true mind of Christendom concerning it. That deliverance was not, in their eyes, a special anomalous transaction, to be set down among the world's curiosities. It was the type and example of all deliverances that had been wrought for nations ever since; of this, the great Redemption of mankind by the baptism and death of the only-begotten Son. All were God's deliverances. In every salvation, little or great, that ever came to an individual, to a family, to a nation, to the universe, He was making a way for his ransomed to pass over, He was commanding the water to stand on the right hand and on the left, He was throwing the horse and the rider into the sea. Is not the whole literature of Christendom, as Dr. Stanley has so well shown in his admirable 'Lectures on the Jewish Church,' leavened with this conviction? Has not this story of the Red Sea given faith to men in sore trials when they needed something else than fictions to rest upon? Yes! The modern method of treating these as mere exceptions in the order of the divine government, not striking and glorious illustrations of it, is a hard, cruel, destructive method. It must lead to such denials as those of Bishop Colenso. We should be thankful for knowing that it does.

Believing that the history of Israel is not a Homeric legend, but a revelation of the Lord of heaven and earth, the Lord of man, I can do justice to the Homeric legends. I can see in them a confession of a divine protection and government in the affairs of men, of a divine inspiration of the thoughts and acts of men. All the world becomes a mere stage, on which men are playing different parts and wearing different masks, without this message concerning a Living Word. With it, the stage becomes a place of real actors. One is in the centre of all, directing all.

But do I care nothing whether Moses or Samuel, or any man whom I have reverenced most, should turn out to be an impostor; not some ancient Descartes, but some ancient Cagliostro? I care immensely! To think of Samuel as some critics think of him, would be as painful to me as to count the dearest friend or kinsman I ever had a rogue. But for that very reason I would not have him snatched away, like a Homeric hero, in a cloud, just when the darts are striking him. I should wish the character of my own friend to undergo investigation, not to be saved from it or to be sustained by any foregone conclusion. I can trust God with His own acts. I can trust Him with the defence of His servants. Let all criticism—the severest—be applied to them. I think they will endure it. I am sure that *He* will be justified when He speaks, and will be clear when He is judged.

Affectionately yours,
F. D. Maurice.

LETTER X.

THE DELUGE.

My dear Friend,

You approach your third question with much timidity. You say that "it is op-"pressing the minds of those who love their "Bibles, and who cling to the infallibility of the "letter of Scripture as the ground of all their "hopes."

I am sure that there are such persons as those whom you describe; I am sure, at least, that there are persons "who love their Bibles," and who yet *think* that "they cling to the infallibi-"lity of the letter of the Scriptures as the ground "of all their hopes." But I cannot admit— after what I have said in previous letters you cannot expect me to admit—that their love for the Bible is identical with this clinging, or is the cause of it. When they confess that the ground of their hopes is *not* the infallibility of the letter of Scripture, but the Rock of Ages, the Living and Eternal Word, I am convinced they will love their Bibles far more; they will receive what their Bibles say with far more simplicity and reverence; the Bible will take the place in their minds of a theory about the Bible; they will care more for David and Isaiah than for M. Gaussen. Thinking, as I do, that their love for the Bible, and that their faith in the Word of God are in unspeakable peril, not from the disturbance of this sandy foundation, but from the fancied security with which they build upon it—being convinced that God is now shaking this foundation for us all, that we may discover that which He has laid—I would approach cautiously and with awe, yet without any cowardly dread, the subject which you propose to me. I am glad to escape from a vague general discussion, in which much may be said and little expressed. Your instance is the best that could be selected. It is important in itself. Any principle which is applicable to it may govern a number of other cases. There are some who " seem to fear that if they once allow the histo-" rical reality of the physical account of the

"Deluge to be called in question, they are guilty "of doubting the word of Him who is Truth."

I do not object to your mode of stating this difficulty. It perhaps conveys your meaning better than any other would convey it. But there is an ambiguity which I think you will now perceive, in the phrase "*historical* reality of "the *physical* account of the Deluge." There may be an historical reality in that which does not in the least correspond with those facts with which the physical student is occupied. It might be true of a deluge covering a very small portion of the earth, that God saved a man and his family from perishing in it; that He gave him a warning of the calamity which was coming before it came; that He taught him how to save his family, and how to save creatures of various kinds, in the same building in which he himself took refuge. All this might be a very simple, child-like narrative of an historical fact, not in the least a legend. This you could easily suppose. But then you will say, 'What is such a narrative 'worth? Who would care the least for it? How 'can a great divine book force such a story upon 'my notice?'

I answer, To the physical student, occupied

with his Cosmos of great continents and islands, a story of this kind would be simply insignificant, simply like any record of the doings of a particular country or province. But I have already started two or three doubts which I wished you to weigh very seriously in your mind. Supposing there is *no* Cosmos but this, what becomes of all that is recorded in *any* human history? Supposing there is *no* Cosmos but this, can you look *this* Cosmos in the face? can you examine it? will you not be crushed by it? Supposing there is *a* Cosmos besides this—supposing there is one in which Man is *not* a mere element—nearly the most insignificant of all its elements—who shall explain that Cosmos to us? Who shall give us a key to the principles of it; to the method in which these principles have unfolded themselves? If there is a Bible, must not this be its object? If there is such a Cosmos—not approached at all by the physical student and his inquiries—do we not want a Bible of this kind?

Now, then, for our immediate topic. In the story of the Deluge of Noah I have that which men in various stages of geographical knowledge, with various degrees of information respecting the relation of this planet to other parts of the universe, have recognized as a message concerning One who punishes men on this earth for their lust and violence, of One who redeems and restores the earth and the human race after He has punished it. This has been the lesson which generation after generation has perceived to lie in it. To have that lesson given in formal didactic words would be nothing. To have it given in some grand legend, surrounded with all kinds of romantic incidents, would not be much. The story of Noah is familiar and prosaic. If you had no associations with the length and breadth of the world to which it referred, you would not be inclined to doubt that it had occurred. Has, then, that length or breadth anything to do with it? I should say, "Absolutely nothing;" if I did not reflect that just in proportion as my thoughts of the earth expand, I must treat the *principle* of this narrative—the *law* of this narrative, as also expanding. If it was true once that God punished men for their lust and violence, it is true still. If it is true that He called forth a righteous man, and preserved him and his family, and other tribes of creatures at that time, it is true that He will do so hereafter; that He has been, and is, and will be the preserver and restorer of the universe and of living things, and of the race which He has made in His image,— a preserver and restorer, let men and animals do what they may to destroy each other and the earth on which they dwell.

I would take, then, the history of this Deluge as I find it given in the book of Genesis. If there are passages in it which assume that more of the earth was covered by the Deluge than modern investigations show can have been covered by it, I would say: 'Either those passages are 'mistaken, or I am mistaken in the interpreta-'tion of them.' Both solutions are possible— both are reasonable. God, if we accept the statement of the Bible, *has* given us an assurance that we shall have His Spirit to guide us into truth. He has not given us a promise or assurance that there shall be no errors in the letter of the Scriptures. If He has, let the passage be produced; let us hear something more than mere inferences as to what men suppose *must* be, —inferences which I hold to be profane and irreverent. But the other alternative is also quite possible. We have made prodigious blunders in our interpretations of Scripture. We have forced it to say things which it has never said, that it may square with our conclusions. It is very hard when we have a certain conception of the earth not to impute that conception to writers who had quite a different conception of it; very hard to remember how much better it may have been that a book which was announcing a moral law, an eternal principle, should meet the various conceptions of men respecting physical things, and that it should demand of us an effort to disengage the permanent truth from these accidents.

And here again we discover from our ecclesiastical documents that it is not the physical fact, but the historical fact, which has impressed itself on the mind and conscience of Christendom. The Baptismal Service uses the Deluge, just as it uses the passage of the Red Sea, without reference to its dimensions, with a simple and direct reference to God's deliverance of man. And quite consistently Bishop Colenso objects to the use of this story, just as he does to the use of the other, because dimensions are for him everything—because a small fact is for him no fact at all. Noah's deluge must have been universal, else why make so much of it? I reply, Because the whole Bible is occupied about small

I

areas, little families, contemptible tribes, shepherds, fishermen, One who was called a carpenter's son, upon whom the Roman soldiers put a purple robe and a crown of thorns in derision—who was nailed to a cross as slaves were. All is consistent. Bulk, as Southey remarked, is sublimity in the mythology of the Hindoos. Goethe saw that the Gospel was, throughout, doing homage to that which man despises for its littleness.

May we not, then, have been weakening instead of strengthening the lesson which has been imparted to age after age by Noah's flood, through our eagerness to make its power consist in its vastness? Perhaps you will say, 'The 'doctrine so stated was very well for the child-'hood of the world; we have outgrown it.' I should hold, on the contrary, that it is more wanted for our manhood than it was wanted for our childhood; that it is more necessary when we are overwhelmed with the mass of physical facts, which are every day accumulating upon us, than it was when only a few here and there had been gathered up, or those few were in the custody of learned men. I remember saying to myself when I read Mr. Wilson's celebrated

Essay, wherein he describes the changes and advances in our knowledge, and compares it with that which the writers of the Bible could have possessed: 'If this is so, how can we breathe if we have not some witness on behalf of humanity, something to save us from sinking under this Atlas load?' I never saw more clearly than from that Essay what would become of us if we were left to the teachers of Physical Science, or if we tried to turn the Bible into a book of Physical Science. And surely it is not in this day that the revelation of a God who permits mutual destruction, and yet is Himself the renovator and restorer of life, is unnecessary either for the physical student, being also a man, or for the divine. The one is confronted with all the facts of this mutual destruction, the other is inclined to turn them into a law, and to hold forth the final discovery and judgment of the Son of Man as that which is to ratify the curse, not to declare the redemption of the universe. Bishop Colenso may tell me that I am a coward and poltroon because I do not inform my people that they have been deceiving themselves in heeding the story of a Deluge. I should deserve this contempt if I ever bade them hold any opinion about the Deluge which I do not hold myself. But I will bear his contempt rather than the stings of which I shall suffer from my conscience, if I took from them what I feel to be an authentic testimony concerning the character and purposes of Him who is the same yesterday, to-day, and for ever—an authentic pledge for the salvation of my race.

I have told you what I think of this particular instance. I believe we owe much to the physical student for warning us off his ground in this matter of the Deluge, for driving us back to our own. We shall hold that far more firmly if we accept the prohibition against trespass as a divine one. I doubt not that theology will owe other debts to those whom it sometimes regards as its enemies. The new inquiries respecting the Antiquity of Man make some people tremble lest the story of Adam in Paradise should be shaken. My own anticipations from those inquiries are altogether hopeful. I know not in what they may issue. But while I have a strong conviction that whatever way the facts go, they will make that simple story more simple and more intelligible to us, and will strip it of a thousand wilful additions, I have a still stronger conviction that we shall never really regard the Second Adam as Him by whom all things were created, and by whom all things consist—as the true Man, the actual image of the Invisible God —till the first Adam occupies quite a different place in our divinity from that which he has occupied for several centuries. The Old Testament speaks of him once after the record of the expulsion from Eden, where Job declares that he *did not hide his sin as Adam.* The New Testament speaks of him twice: once in the fifth chapter of the Epistle to the Romans, to call him *the type of Him that was to come,* to say that '*not as the offence, so also is the free gift;*' the other in the Epistle to the Corinthians, to declare that *as in Adam all die, so in Christ shall all be made alive; that the first man was made a living soul, the last a quickening spirit.* Turn to any book of systematic divinity, and you would suppose Adam's fall was the subject of the Bible, the very ground of Law and Gospel. Surely such a divinity needs reformation. Thanks to the physical student if in anywise he helps the Reformation forward. He will not help it forward, nor promote his own cause either, by diminishing our reverence for the Bible, or by leading us to think of it as less really a word of God than we have been wont to think it. As reverence takes place of the idolatry which destroys reverence, we shall learn from it to reverence all God's voices to us in the history of man and the life of nature. The living Word of God will indeed be owned as the Light of men, the source of all light whatever in their hearts and reasons. We shall look upon the facts of the universe as His facts. That we may investigate them, and grow in knowledge of Him, we shall bid our noisy disputatious intellects keep silence before Him.

Ever yours affectionately,

F. D. MAURICE.

LETTER XI.

CURRENT PHRASES IN THIS CONTROVERSY.

MY DEAR FRIEND,

You refer to several phrases which are disturbing many minds at this time. The first is *Inspiration*. I have not thought it needful to discuss the meaning of that word: our Church Prayers speak of it sufficiently; our Church Articles are wisely, piously, and significantly silent upon it. The subject is one for prayer, not for definitions. If we pray, we must confess that Inspiration for which our Collects continually entreat. We must suppose that we cannot think, believe, act without it; we must acknowledge that all wisdom, illumination, power to will and to do, proceed from the Divine Spirit. We dare not define or limit His operations; we only know that He is the good Spirit, the Holy Spirit; that only good can come from Him;

that He gives us insight to perceive evil, and strength to resist it.

That holy men, then, of old spoke by the inspiration of God, that the same inspiration enables us to know what they said, to have any clear understanding of any kind: this has been the faith of the Church at all times. To control it by theories of ours is to undermine it; to say that inspiration is confined to the writers of the Bible, is formally and directly to contradict those writers; to determine in what measures they or any other men have possessed inspiration, is to tell Him who breathes where He listeth how *we* suppose He must breathe or ought to breathe. I believe we should repent deeply of having entertained so profane a thought. He knows what inspiration is fitting for each of His servants; we cannot. A denial of the promise of the Spirit, a disbelief that He has been given, and that He dwells with us for ever, is surely latent in such speculations. How is this denial, this disbelief compatible with our acceptance of the most direct declarations of the New Testament?

On the other hand, I have spoken at some length on the expression "*Word of God.*" It seems to me that we clergymen should very seriously apply ourselves to the question, "What "sense does this expression convey to us when "we read the Scriptures? Have what we call "the different senses of it no relation to each "other? Is the use of it by St. John a mere "figurative accidental use; or does that interpret "all the other applications of it? Has it found "its meaning till we come to that meaning?" If we do give ourselves steadily to this inquiry, I suspect that many of the complaints which the Laity make of us will be found to originate, not, as they often suspect, in our too rigid adherence to our own peculiar phraseology, but in our carelessness about it, in the low and narrow signification which we attach to it. If we had been more faithful in listening to the testimonies of Scripture respecting the Word of God, we should have embarrassed them much less with cruel demands upon them to deny the lessons which God gives them in their consciences, in human history, in the world of nature, out of deference, or supposed deference, to the letter of the Bible. We must begin with paying some respect to the letter ourselves, where it is distinct and most uniform, before we call upon other men to follow it in points which are trivial, and merely accidental to its main purpose.

There is a third expression which has occupied us much, which, I am persuaded, must occupy us all continually, if we would see our way through the difficulties that beset us on every side. I began by confessing a difference with you as to the meaning of *Revelation*. You will now see, I think, why I insisted so much upon that difference. The confusion which exists in all our minds between the mere book and the Revelations whereof the book speaks, is the source of very many of our confusions. "To what are we to trust?" this demand I hear continually; you yourself have made it. 'Is it to the letter of the Bible? But 'who is to tell us what that says, what that 'signifies? Is it to some tradition or general 'consent of the Church? But the Church fled 'from the tradition and consent to an infallible 'human interpreter, and was driven back from 'that infallible interpreter to the Bible itself, 'as the great deliverer from bewildering decrees 'which the Laity could not understand; and 'which weakened and depraved their consci- 'ences, if through the help of some confessor or 'director they were changed from mere general

'dogmas into maxims of individual conduct.
' Must we fall back in hopelessness upon this
' scheme, weighed in the balance and found want-
'ing by Englishmen three centuries ago, not
' proved to be more satisfactory or more uniting
' by any recent experience? Or shall the letter
' of the Bible be claimed by every sect or school
' that is uppermost as a weapon for persecuting
' and slaying all other sects and schools? Or
' shall a combination of sects and schools use it
' for restraining examination into the facts of
' God's universe?'

Is GOD the Revealer? Greeks, Romanists, Protestants, all say that He is. The Creeds affirm it; the existence of the Church implies it. *Can* He reveal? Can He make us know what He is; how we are related to Him; what we are? This *is* the question. If it is resolved negatively, ' He *cannot* reveal; there is some-
· thing in the constitution of our minds which
' makes it impossible that He should show us
' what He is, what we are, how we are related
' to Him,' then I do not see that it signifies much how we settle the question about the Bible, tradition, the infallible human authority. All are equally deceiving us. All are pretending to tell

us something which they cannot tell us. All are merely repeating phrases which begin in nothing, and end in nothing. We have, then, only to ask which party plays its tricks best, which shuffles the false cards most dexterously.

I believe that the Bible and the Creeds, the holiest traditions of the Church in all ages, the holiest Greeks, Latins, Protestants in all ages, are agreed in this one testimony: that God has revealed, and does reveal, to men that which they want to know; that He only does, or can, reveal anything. Every Reformation has been a protest on behalf of this principle: an effort to shake off, not faith, but denials, not authority, but the rebellion of Popes, of Doctors, of sects, of a religious world, against the Divine authority: a determination to recover the Divine teaching which had been lost. If Bishop Colenso had made this protest, this effort, this determination, with what joy would some of us have followed in his steps! I have expressed in a former letter the pleasure which his preface gave me, because it echoed the words of that prophecy which is read as the Epistle for the Tuesday before Easter,—*Who is among you that feareth the Lord, that obeyeth His servants, that walketh in darkness, and hath no light; let him trust in the name of the Lord, and stay himself upon his God.* If he had gone on to exhort us, one and all, to abstain from *kindling a fire and compassing ourselves with sparks,* not to invent theories which shut out God's light from ourselves and from other men—how should we have listened to him as to a father in God, owning that dignity in him all the more readily because he had none of the dignity of earthly greatness and wealth to mix with it and confuse it! But he has kindled these sparks; he has invented theories; he has taught us to distrust God's past revelations, those which are the preparations for His revelation of His Only Begotten Son, those which are our encouragements to hope for the perfect Revelation of Him when all our partial glimpses shall be completed, all our dim anticipations satisfied.

To such guidance we cannot commit ourselves. But every fresh disappointment of this kind, every confutation of any dreams we might have formed of earthly leaders, are only reasons for more entirely trusting the cause of God's Church and of His Truth to Himself. Whatever becomes of our lights, His will shine more and more to the perfect day. And that Light, I am convinced, will illuminate the path of the physical as well as of the moral student. The Heavens shall declare the glory of God, when man is taught that he was made of the dust of earth, that he is meant to bear the image of the Eternal God.

Ever yours affectionately,

F. D. MAURICE.

LETTER XII.

THE LAW COURTS.—THE PEOPLE OF GOD.—
ETERNAL PUNISHMENT.

My dear Friend,

It will occur to you to ask—in fact, you have asked—How do these interpretations of yours accord with the decisions of our Ecclesiastical Courts? I am not so careful about that question as about some others; but I will answer it frankly, certainly without considering how far the answer may affect my own security. In the cases of Mr. Rowland Williams and Mr. Wilson we saw a most conscientious, able, and kind-hearted Judge perplexed between the claims of modern zeal for the Bible and the authority of old books, compiled in times which reverenced the Bible far more than we do, and were supposed to have guarded its rights more jealously. Ultimately he decided, in deference to those authorities, that clergymen possess a liberty in the investigation of the Scriptures which the public opinion of the day considers perilous to the Scriptures, and which *is* perilous to the maxims that this public opinion has canonized.

I draw this distinction. I feel it to be one of unspeakable importance. Has Dr. Lushington, by his decree in these cases, really weakened the authority of the Bible, or has he only shaken some notions about the Bible which interfere with its rightful authority, and with the understanding of its contents? Holding the latter opinion, I only regret the degree of sanction which the Courts have given to our current notions.

I have contended already that Bishop Colenso's offences against the Bible can be traced to his too credulous acceptance of a prevalent theory about the Bible. I have hinted at another cause of his alienation from the Old Testament. It has affected so many who have gone in his direction, that I wish to speak of it a little more at large. The Old Testament speaks everywhere of "the people of God." A whole people—the nation of Israel—is declared to be dear to the

Most High; to be chosen by Him; to be cherished in spite of trangressions; to be loved with an everlasting love; to be sought after in its wanderings; to have the hope of ultimate repentance and restoration. There are godly men among the people and ungodly. The former may be a little flock—a remnant. The latter may be very numerous. They may be seated in high places. But the godly, however few, are those who believe that God cares for the *whole nation;* that He is guiding it; that He means to preserve it and bless it. The ungodly, however numerous, are those who distrust the God of Abraham and of Israel; who make separate gods; who cultivate a religion of their own.

Now, the phrase "people of God" has been distorted into a sense the very reverse of this. There are certain evidences in certain persons that they truly believe—believe things which other men do not believe—believe in a way in which other men do not believe. These persons are said to be the people of God. Their belief invests them with that character. *They* are loved with an everlasting love. *Their* transgressions are blotted out. *They* are to be brought to an endless felicity. Devout men become aware of the contradictions which this theory involves, of its dangerous permissions, of its cruel exclusions, of the security which it holds out to insincere profession, of the despair which it causes to humble Christians. They feel that it withdraws them from trust in God's grace—to trust in their own signs of grace. They feel that it leads them to credit themselves with qualities which, in their prayers, they confess that they want. They become impatient of it. They long to overthrow barriers which it has set up between them and their fellow-creatures. But they never dream that they might recover a sounder position by reconsidering the language of the book from which theirs has been adopted. They have been effectually cut off from the simple signification of its records. Its national phraseology is unintelligible to them. They suppose it to be narrow, because their own minds have been narrowed. They retain a certain notion that religious men, or spiritual men, are the favourites of Heaven. They only alter their definition of religious men and spiritual men. They discover religious and spiritual instincts in Greeks, Brahmins, Mahometans. There must be such if the Bible is true; if there is a Word of God speaking to men; if men everywhere have been seeking after God as St. Paul says that they have. But those who are suddenly awakened to the perception of this fact make a strange use of it. The intuitions of heathens are turned to the disparagement of the book which explains and justifies them. They are made a plea for the indulgence of that very exclusiveness against which they are invoked. A refined religion is put in place of a Gospel to all people. The Righteous God, who hates idols that divide and degrade men, is regarded as a mere hard conception of Hebrew theology. A God who cares for a nation is inconsistent with an expanded philanthropy. So the way is closed to the revelation of a Son of God, who in his own person contends with the enemies of mankind; to the revelation of a Father, who in that Son sees and loves mankind, and wills that all should come to the knowledge of His truth.

Thus, the habit of mind which pervades our English Christianity—which has penetrated so deeply into the heart of our religion, that we all, in our different ways, exhibit the tokens of it—is responsible for that weakening of faith in the *Old* Covenant which is charged upon Bishop Colenso, and which the Bishop of Durham affirms to be characteristic of our modern literature. Thus, that same exclusive temper, which leads so many to complain of our Catechism for claiming all baptized men as children of God, is driving numbers to seek in a vague philosophical universalism something better than the finished salvation which is announced, and the restitution of all things which is promised, in the *New* Covenant.

I am bound to make these remarks, even if they are a digression—and I think they are not—from our main subject, because, in a passage of his commentary on the Epistle to the Romans, Bishop Colenso has referred to me with much kindness and with most graceful modesty, saying that he had once declared his dissent from an opinion which I had expressed respecting the possibility of good to those who leave this world in an evil state; and that, upon more mature reflection, he was inclined to withdraw that dissent. I should be very base if I shrank from far more than the disgrace to which such an allusion may expose me. What he has embodied in the form of a charitable hope I have put into words which directly contravene the sentence of that excellent judge who has granted so much latitude to the critics of Scripture. That judge has said that the words "everlasting punishment" or "everlasting fire," in the Athanasian Creed must be taken to denote an endless destruction of certain persons in a future state. I have said that I cannot give those adjectives this sense, unless I take eternal life to mean merely an endless future felicity; unless I regard the Eternal God, not as One who is, and was, and is to come, but only as a future Being. The whole New Testament is for me a revelation of eternal life, the life of God; a redemption from eternal death, the death of which only a spirit is capable, the death of separation from God, of attachment to evil. If I preached that there could be no deliverance from eternal death, I should be preaching that no sinner can be raised from darkness to light, from the power of Satan to God. That this deliverance can only take place before the grave closes upon us I am told is the doctrine of Scripture. When I ask for the passages, I am referred to those very words, 'eternal' and 'everlasting,' against the contraction and perversion of which I am protesting. Or I am reminded of an undying worm, which, I am sure, does and must prey upon the conscience of every evil man; the question being whether he must necessarily remain evil. In every case I plead, not for evasions of Christ's words, but for the strictest explanation that can be given of them, according to the letter, the context, and the analogy of Scripture. In every case I complain of the popular interpretation, not for its severity, but for the practical laxity which its fierceness engenders; I complain because it deters from no crime, and cultivates the despair which is the cause of ten thousand crimes.

Instead, therefore, of flying from Christ to some dreams of a possible felicity for man without Christ, I turn to Him as the Friend and Head of all men; I turn to Him from the torments of my own accusing conscience, from the hopelessness which the sight of the world's evils is always causing me, and which no thoughts about nature, or civilization, or the progress of the species, or the power of man's will, are able to dissipate. If I had not believed in the revelation of the Eternal God of Righteousness to the poor shepherd in the bush that burnt and was not consumed, I should never have learnt to feel as I do feel about the abuse of the word 'eternal.' If I did not accept the records of the Jewish nation as veritable history, I should never have had a glimpse of the patience of God with the human race, or of His purpose towards it. If I did not perceive that every Jew was a righteous man just in proportion as he counted his nation righteous, in spite of its transgressions and infidelities, I should not confess that the whole race of man is righteous in its King and High Priest, and that no one of us can boast of a private self-righteousness, but must abdicate all title to such a distinction if he would be a true man and a servant of God. My strong convictions on this subject, therefore, increase my dislike to Bishop Colenso's doctrines respecting the Old Testament. Nevertheless, I cannot deny that these convictions are more at strife with ecclesiastical law, as it has been recently expounded, than any of his doctrines are, and that I am far more deeply committed on the question of eternal punishment than he is.

On the other hand, I have no doubt that the popularity of Bishop Colenso's work with a certain class of readers is mainly owing to the opinion—how widely diffused I dare not guess—that the Bible is a book which sentences an immense majority of the creatures whom it declares God has made in his image, to hopeless destruction. A less amount of arithmetic than he possesses would induce men to throw off the incubus of an authority which they suppose exists to curse them. I do not believe that the clergy will abate his influence, or that of any person who attacks any part of the Bible history, except by bearing witness that the book, according to the simple letter of it as it presents itself to a wayfarer, is directly the reverse of that which laymen, judging from our discourses, have taken it to be. We must say plainly, "God is declared in every page of the Bible to be a God of Salvation. He is that, and only that. If we suppose Him to be anything else, we confound Him with the Devil." The Ecclesiastical Courts cannot bear this testimony. Yet they cannot be without their use, for nothing in God's universe is without use. These Courts may teach modern clergymen that their ancestors left us a freedom which they would take away; that lay Judges are fairer than clerical Judges, because they are occupied with subjects to which criminal jurisdiction is applicable, and we invoke it for subjects to which it has been proved inapplicable; that those who try to turn this weapon against their brethren will one day find it piercing themselves; that no fear of it must make us false to God, or lead us to suppress the Gospel with which he has entrusted us for his creatures.

Affectionately yours,

F. D. Maurice.

LETTER XIII.

OPINIONS OF BISHOPS ON THE FOUNDATION OF OUR HOPES.

My dear Friend,

I thought I had said all that I had need to say in the Claims of the Bible and of Science. But a letter has appeared during the last week in the newspapers, signed by the Bishop of Natal, which leads me to reopen our correspondence. It refers to a speech said to have been delivered by the Bishop of Manchester at a meeting of the Church Missionary Society. If we may believe the reporter of that speech, the Bishop of Manchester declared that the very foundations of our faith—the very basis of our hopes—the very nearest and dearest of our consolations are taken from us when one line of that sacred volume, on which we base everything, is said to be unfaithful or untrustworthy. As the Bishop of Natal had said that many lines of the Bible are unfaithful and untrustworthy, Bishop Lee added that there was no language befitting a gentleman and a Christian which he could not use in his condemnation. The Bishop of Natal immediately calls upon his Right Reverend Brother to say whether he rests his faith, his hopes, and his consolations on the truth of the passage in the eleventh chapter of Leviticus, which decrees, on the authority of the Almighty, that the hare is not to be eaten because he cheweth the cud, but divideth not the hoof. Bishop Colenso has asked Professor Owen whether the hare chews the cud, and has received an answer in the negative.

Grievous as this conflict between two fathers of the Church must be to every member of the Church, it throws a light upon the subject of those Letters which we cannot afford to lose. I hope I shall speak with the respect which I feel for their office, and for them individually. But there are duties which every Presbyter owes to himself and to his calling, and with the performance of these that respect must not interfere.

I need not say that Bishop Lee's proposition is directly and essentially at variance with the principles which I have maintained in my letters to you. I have acknowledged one foundation as laid for us all. That foundation is *not* the letter of any book. That foundation, being our Lord Jesus Christ himself, could not be shaken if the whole Bible were taken from us. I say this on the authority of the Bible. I should contradict the Bible if I said otherwise. Supposing the Bishop of Manchester exacts from the clergy of his diocese a confession similar to that which he made at the Church Missionary meeting, I, were I one of those clergy, should be silenced. I could not preach the Gospel which has been committed to me—I could not accept the creeds I have accepted—and also take a pledge which appears to me inconsistent with both.

But you will perceive also, from my Letters, and from the statement I have just made, how utterly unpalatable and offensive to me must be the reply of the Bishop of Natal to the Bishop of Manchester. If ever there was an occasion when a moral principle was at stake,—when a protest, if it was made at all, should have been made on moral grounds,—when nothing should have been allowed to rest on a point of scholarship, or on the question of what might or might not be an error in natural history—this was that occasion.

If ever there was a question which demanded the most serious treatment,—about which every temptation to a joke, however lawful on certain occasions, should have been resisted—this was that question. The Bishop of Natal has made his cause depend upon the accuracy of his knowledge of the force given by the writer of the book of Leviticus to the words which we translate "chewing the cud." He has addressed himself, not to the reason or conscience of his readers, but to their sense of the ridiculous. He may justify himself by saying, "Why did you drive me to this? Why did you put so grave a matter upon such an issue?" But is that justification available in a higher court? Is the extravagance of one man a plea for another to be frivolous, and to cultivate frivolity, upon topics of the deepest human interest?

But I have a more important objection to this course. The Bishop's sneering allusion to Almighty God as the author of the law about eating a hare, belongs to his whole conception of the Pentateuch and its legislation. That this legislation contains minute regulations concerning the health and habits of an Eastern people, and affirms those regulations to be divine, is for him an evident absurdity. He knows that it sounds like an absurdity to a number of his countrymen. He can always invoke this feeling to his side; as a mere special pleader, that is his wisest and safest course. But I am convinced that this sentiment is as vulgar as it is widely diffused. It is connected with the notion of God as a very great Being, who does not care about little things. Such a notion is exceedingly natural to us all. I find it *so* natural to myself, and so destructive of what is best in me, that I know scarcely a stronger proof of the veracity of the Scripture records than this—that they educate me, as no other books educate me, out of this temper of mind; that they compel me to believe that God *does* care for the sanitary condition, for the bodily circumstances, of the people of my land and of every land. Statutes which were adapted to the condition of an Eastern people, to a race coming out of slavery into freedom, out of a nomadic condition into fixed habitations, fifteen hundred years before Christ, or as many more as chronologers like to fix, may be bad for our condition. But those modern legislators who think they want no divine guidance in judging what is needful for the complications of a civilized State—those who suppose that this can be ascertained by following the newspapers and public opinion—appear to me less wise than the early legislators of all lands, who thought that to provide for a people, or to govern a people, was an altogether amazing work, for which they needed at every step a teaching from above. All of them had this conviction, and expressed it; but most of them sought help from other than righteous guidance—from tricks and enchantments, from hereditary titles or their own cunning. The Jewish legislator, referring all his wisdom, all the sanction of his laws, to the unseen Deliverer and Ruler, sinking himself altogether, exhibiting the sins of his family and tribe, conferred a blessing upon Israelites which we can only appreciate by considering its effects on those who accepted his words most strictly. Why did David take the shewbread for the wants of his soldiers, when that bread was only for the priests? Because he felt that he was subject to a divine legislator; that God, and not Moses, had consecrated that bread; that the decree had, therefore, a meaning beyond its letter; that the God who cared for the meanest wants of men would have him despise the letter to obey the sense. The Israelites were raised out of superstition by that sentence—'The Lord God hath said,' 'The Lord God gives this command,' which the Bishop of Natal would ridicule, as the cause of superstition.

Afterwards, in the days of letter worship, these statutes were turned into pleas for the basest superstition. Every commandment of God was overlaid by the tradition of the elders; and then commandments, traditions, and all—the traditions often stifling and destroying the commandments—became a yoke which neither the Jews of the latest age, nor their fathers, were able to bear. But while the Scriptures, in which the Pharisees sought their life, were used as reasons for not coming to Him of whom the Scriptures testified as the source of life—the witness against this tyranny and usurpation of the letter was not a *denial* that God had given the commandments—the particular and general, the little as well as the great—but the *assertion* that He had, and that He lived, and that He could fulfil the meaning of them, and that He was abrogating the letter in order to fulfil the meaning of them.

I find, then, in this controversy of the two

Bishops, a remarkable illustration of the danger to which we are exposed on both sides; of the evil into which we shall certainly fall if either prevails against the other. Unbelief in the Divine Word is as much the disease of the Bishop of Natal as of the Bishop of Manchester. In both there is a denial of Him who is, and who was, and who is to come; of His government over the ages that are gone; of His government over us now. I say this is the *disease* of both, because it is the disease of the age, yours and mine. I do not say there is not a *health* in both which is fighting against the disease. I am sure there is. I am sure that in his heart of hearts the Bishop of Manchester believes—probably far more firmly and consistently than I do—that Christ Himself is the Rock upon which all our hopes and consolations must rest. I am sure that the Bishop of Natal—he has said so in words, and they are the evident expression of his profoundest conviction—casts himself upon God as his only refuge from his own feebleness and contradictions, and from the evils which he sees about him. But then comes the solemn question which each of us must ask for himself—which will perhaps be answered in thunders and lightnings more terrible than those of Sinai for the whole Church,—" How shall the health in me, how shall the health in every one of us, conquer the disease?"

I have put this question to my own conscience; and thus much, at least, of a reply I have found to it:—' So far as I magnify my own opinions—so far as I desire that they should triumph—so far as I desire that the opinions which are opposed to them should be put down— so far I am strengthening the disease in myself and in my contemporaries; I am weakening my own health and theirs.' Let me not stay for a moment in generals. I will apply my principle at once to the case before us.

I repudiate the maxim of the Bishop of Manchester; I repudiate the maxim of the Bishop of Natal. Ought I, then, to desire that I could get the Bishop of Manchester removed from his diocese, or pronounced guilty of heresy? Our desires are not tied by improbabilities, so I have a right to consider whether this would be a legitimate *wish*, utterly unable as I might be to effect it. I say it would *not* be a legitimate wish. I say, if I could get rid of that expression of opinion which the Bishop has put forth—if I could hinder any simple clergyman, any head of a diocese, from using his language, I should be injuring the Church by doing so. My reason is this. If what I maintain is good for anything, it is good on this ground; it is good as a protest against an attempt to substitute the letters of a book, or the theories of a man about the letters of a book, for Him of whom the book speaks; it is good as a declaration that Christ is the centre of His Church, the bond of its fellowship, and that no opinions about Him, or about any other matter, are or can be the centres of it, or the bonds of its fellowship. But if I could suppress Bishop Lee's opinions and proclaim mine, I should be contradicting, ridiculously contradicting, my own principle. *I* should be enthroning an opinion; *I* should be dethroning Christ.

Well, but if this principle is true as to one Bishop, it is true as to the other. Their opinions both scandalize me; I could not hold either and be a minister of the English Church. But, thank God! I am not the standard for either of them. I am not the least a judge what opinions are compatible in them with the most living faith in God's Word. I have expressed my conviction that they have that living faith; that I should be the better if I could increase mine by that which is in either of them. And, after all, this is not what we have to consider chiefly. Their inward personal faith is open to another scrutiny than ours. But is it beneficial for the faith of the Church, for the faith once delivered to the Saints, for that confession of the Divine Name of which I spoke in a former letter, that either of them should be restrained from entertaining or from delivering those private and contradictory judgments? Everything which I see in the world, illustrating that which I read in the Bible, convinces me that it is not beneficial. That Name will, as I believe, be recognized at last as above us all and beneath us all; as the consummation of all we can hope for; as the eternal basis of society. But if we would reach this result, we must walk in the way in which God is leading us; we must not choose a way of our own. We have all been choosing ways of our own. We have all fancied that we can provide better for the safety and well-being of the Church than God has provided for it. He permits diversities of opinion in His ministers; we have tried to crush them. We have done it, no doubt, for His glory; there is no crime that we have not committed for His glory. But how is His glory served by the substitution of one opinion or another for Himself?

It is hard to persuade any man that this course is a mistaken and an ungodly one; very hard indeed; since all the demonstrations of God's providence, all our complaints of the impossibility of getting our own opinions established and other men's proscribed, have not persuaded us. There is not one Church—not one Sect—which has not had a glimpse of this truth, which has not asserted it manfully in hours of trial and persecution; there is not one which has not set at nought the maxim learnt in the school of suffering when it has had the opportunity of punishing its opponent and exalting itself. Why? Because in adversity Churches and Sects, like individuals, believe in God. In prosperity they believe in themselves, and sink into Atheism. The English Church is now on its trial whether her belief in opinions which is rampant, or her belief in God which is certainly not dead, shall prove the stronger. For my own part, feeling how strong my fondness for my opinions is, and how weak my faith in the Living Lord and Judge is,

I can only ask Him that I may never be indulged with the chance of crushing any opinions that are contrary to mine ; that I may, by any discipline He knows to be best, be raised above them, and taught to confide in Him.

To speak, however, of our general duty. Now that men who are above us, whom we are bound to respect, not for their worldly rank but for their spiritual position, are divided from each other—are saying as much against each other 'as Christians and gentlemen may say'—does it not become absolutely necessary, if we would uphold the cause of Order, if we would not have the most outrageous spectacles continually brought before our eyes, to accept our position; to admit that we cannot by the aid of any courts, common or ecclesiastical, coerce opinions or establish opinions; to believe that God is King, actually, and not nominally; to believe that His Court of Appeal is never closed against those who do not anticipate its decisions, or try to enforce their own? *"Shall not we gather up the tares?"* ask the servants. "No," answers the Householder with unmistakeable clearness, *"lest, while ye gather up the tares, ye root up the wheat also with them. Let both grow together till the har-*

vest." I suspect the Householder knows better than we do. I suspect that he does not mean us to make the selection, which he says we are incompetent to make. If our Bishops could have rooted up the tares that grew on the rich soil which the spades of the evangelical teachers of the last century turned up, what an extirpation they would have made! What wheat, dear to the Husbandman inestimable to us, would have perished! If they could have torn up the tares which were sown plentifully during the High Church movement, how wise they would have deemed themselves! But what wheat would they not have destroyed with the tares! And who can tell how much the tares have been multiplied in both cases by the refusal to confess the wheat? Must this new movement only lead to a repetition of the same errors; only give occasion for the same repentance?

But we cannot blame the Bishops. They have responded to our cries; they have made themselves the organs of our fears; of our contempt; I must add, of our unbelief. If they have exposed themselves to lay censure by holding out the threat of legal proceedings and anticipating the decision in such proceedings, it is our impatience which has caused that indifference to justice. If they have strangely mingled appeals to the conscience with their threats, and have made whispers of affection public through the newspapers, they have but echoed the dissonant notes and the confused sentiments of their spiritual children. They have not too much exalted their office. They have thought too humbly of it. What blessings many of us have derived from their private counsels and encouragements when they have assumed a right to correct us; to rebuke our want of faith and charity; to show a more excellent way than our own! When they speak publicly or collectively, that the world may know what they are saying, we lose all these benefits. We are flattered in our weaknesses; comforted with the assurances of our sound belief and extensive knowledge; confirmed in our animosities; instructed how to conceal them in soft and tender phrases.

Oh! will not the clergy feel that they want Bishops, not as their servants, but as their guides and overseers; in very deed as their Fathers? Will not those Fathers believe that they are responsible, not to us, not to a public opinion, but to a "Father in heaven" for their care of us, for helping us to rise above slavery to private or to public opinion? At all events that Father lives. We may betake ourselves to Him. We may commit ourselves, the Bible, the Church, to His keeping.

Affectionately yours,
F. D. MAURICE.

POSTSCRIPT.

The last number of the 'Edinburgh Review' which has just appeared contains two articles which bear directly upon the subject of these letters, and which are sure to be read extensively. The first, entitled "The Bible and the Church," is equally reasonable and devout. It exhibits very strikingly the contradictions into which those have fallen and must fall who are determined to rest the authority of the Bible upon a theory of their own respecting its inspiration and infallibility, when they might appeal to the actual authority which it has exercised over generations of men in the most civilized countries of the earth. This article, I trust, will not be read chiefly as an exposure of the weakness of those who assume the patronage of the Scriptures—though that weakness deserves to be exposed, because it is accompanied with so much irreverence, so much presumption, often so much cruelty—but far more as a vindication of the faith of those who look up to the Scriptures as their teachers; who turn to them from all their own theories and speculations, as their helpers in every time of need; who derive from them every day fresh lessons of humility for themselves, and of charity towards their fellow-men.

The second article, "On Mr. Huxley's Place of Man in Nature," is one which I should not venture to notice, seeing that I am utterly incompetent to enter into the argument between the reviewer and the subject of his criticism, but for one passage which occurs in the latter part of it (page 568). The scientific objections to Mr. Darwin's and Mr. Huxley's theories having been urged (I doubt not, with much ability), an effort is made to strengthen them by the insinuation that these opinions must lead to materialism and atheism.

The *odium theologicum* is, in this case at all events, brought into the controversy, not by a defender of the Scriptures, but by a champion of what is commonly called Natural Theology. Such a person, it seems to me, may be well excused for the fears which he expresses. If those fears interfere inconveniently with the investigation of facts, they are still so serious —the loss of everything spiritual and divine to one who feels that he is a man as well as a student of physics would be so tremendous— that I cannot blame him (even while I feel that he is dishonouring truth, and that he may be doing a great injustice and injury to sincere and worthy men) for hindering search by denouncing its possible results. But I do say that a man who accepts the Scriptures of the Old and New Testament, and not Paley's 'Natural Theology' as his Bible; who never dreams of rising "from nature up to nature's God;" who starts with the belief in God as his Father, has no right to cherish those apprehensions, or to indulge in those insinuations. Claiming for Man a place *above* nature—a direct relation to God through a Mediator—a mansion in a house which is eternal in the heavens—he cannot be anxious about the place which Man may be found to hold *in* nature. As I have urged already, we want only free room and courage to tell men that they are made in God's image, and that He seeks to raise them to that image; we cannot wish to check any inquiry respecting that lower bestial image, the signs of which are palpable enough in every one of us. Our physical students may find, at last, that those who assert most strongly the 'Claims of the Bible' are the least likely to deny or to endanger the 'Claims of Science.'

April 17, 1863.

My dear Maurice,

I cannot regret that I have given you the trouble of writing the series of Letters you have now closed. Though you modestly expect but a small audience, many who may have been influenced by Bishop Colenso's evident earnestness, or by his acuteness, will, I am sure, be helped, by what you have written, to assume for themselves a higher standard of historical truth than his, and a more just estimate of the bearing of physical facts on human history.

Whether your anonymous correspondent agrees with all you have said may well be a matter of indifference to your readers, who will form their own judgment on the value of your answers to my questions.

If I ask your leave to add a few supplementary words of my own, I must incur the risk of being compared to the country organist who told Handel that, as he could not play out the lingering audience, he would play them out for him. As, however, I wrote to you because I thought you could best answer questions which I knew were engaging the minds of some friends of mine engaged in various secular occupations, it may not be altogether useless if I shortly put together some practical reflections suggested by the perusal of your letters, and by communications, received since I wrote to you, from another friend well able to deal with such questions.

I must, however, guard myself by again saying that, influenced partly by private considerations, still more by a sense of what befits me as a layman writing to a clergyman, I express no opinion publicly on the conduct of the Bishop of Natal, nor on the censures directed against him. I confine myself to the facts and arguments brought forward in the present controversy. Those, however, who have means of judging of the effects on the laity of what is passing, may regret, as a matter of expediency, much which they have no power to influence, and no call to criticize.

I have only to ask that the truth may not

suffer from the supposition that a dry statement of mere opinion proceeds from cold indifference to the great issues at stake.

I proceed, then, to remark shortly on the following points:—

1. The order in which the questions on this controversy ought to be treated.

2. The connection of the Old Testament with the New.

3. The critical results of Bishop Colenso's publications.

4. Their bearing on the authority of the "Word of God."

5. Their bearing on clerical obligations.

I. First, too much stress cannot be laid on the principle you have pointed out as underlying the order and mutual connection of the questions arising out of the present controversy. We should not begin with the Pentateuch, and postpone the study of the Gospel till we have settled our difficulties about the Old Testament; but, as you say, "we profess to believe in Christ, from that point we should start" (page 91). The Dean of Ely, better known by the name of Harvey Goodwin, as a practical mathematician not inferior to Bishop Colenso, and, like yourself, the associate and friend of working laymen, in his work "On the Doctrines and Difficul-"ties of the Christian Faith, contemplated from "the standing ground afforded by the Catholic "Doctrine of the Being of our Lord Jesus Christ; "being the Hulsean Lectures for the year 1856," has, as you are no doubt aware, placed the question on a basis which may come home alike to the man of science and to the scholar.

Starting from the "point of view which forms the basis of Bishop Butler's" great storehouse of principles, he propounds, in substance, this question—Given as our data the complicated facts of our moral and physical existence, let us assume, as a possible hypothesis, the Being of Christ. Does the assumption of this hypothesis explain the phenomena and solve the difficulties? Assume the contrary of this hypothesis, is there any other solution? From this point of view, let us contemplate ancient and modern history —the progress of science—the progress, if you will, of revelation—the difficulties attendant on the language, inspiration, and authority of the Sacred Scriptures. Does not the hypothesis bring the various phenomena into harmonious consistency? But, it will be said, it is only an hypothesis.

Now let us look at the facts clearly within our knowledge. Before we plunge into the difficulties of books believed to have been written fifteen hundred years before Christ—that is, a thousand years before the birth of the Father of History—let this be remembered: The Gospel history was written in the blaze of the most brilliant age of literature; when the intercourse between educated men in all parts of the civilized world was more intimate than at any period before or after, up to our own age. It has been well observed by a great historian that the death of Julius Cæsar is not so well attested as the death and resurrection of Jesus Christ. Let this fact be well pondered before any man allows himself to be entangled by difficulties about ancient records, or by arguments against miracles. It is not beside the question to remark, in passing, that Bishop Colenso raises no difficulties about miracles as such. He who believes the Resurrection may approach the whole question of more ancient miracles without anxiety. Let that central fact be looked at on its own merits.

Next, it is well to bear in mind that whatever

may be too truly said about the defect of Hebrew scholarship amongst us, there is no nation on earth that can claim superiority to England in masculine Greek scholarship, or historical research. I do not mean to deny the vast industry and critical acumen of the Germans, or the consummate clearness of the French; but I am confident that the critical judgment of England, solid and acute, may face the world. Now, this very Gospel history, and the history of the Acts of the Apostles and of St. Paul, have been submitted to a searching criticism and examination such as hardly any other subject has received. All that has been said is well known in England, and accessible to hundreds—nay, thousands—of educated laymen. If the same methods of inquiry be applied to the Old Testament, and if the result should be to modify some of our preconceived ideas, we know enough of what can be said about the New Testament to feel no fear that any truth which may be elicited will affect the grounds of Christian faith or practice.

II. The connection between Christianity and the details recorded in the patriarchal and Jewish history appears to be liable to misconception. It opens, as I intimated in the third question which I addressed to you, a solemn subject, which needs cautious and reverent handling. I am not about to go further into that question than you have gone. But I think it may render some service to direct the attention of your readers to a passage in Paley's 'Evidences,' which has been pointed out to me by a friend, namely, part iii. chap. 3. After premising that "our Saviour assumes the Divine origin of "the Mosaic institution," and "recognizes the "prophetic character of many of their ancient "writers," Paley says: "So far, therefore, we "are bound, as Christians, to go. But to make "Christianity answerable with its life for the cir- "cumstantial truth of each separate passage of "the Old Testament, the genuineness of every "book, the information, fidelity, and judgment "of every writer in it, is to bring, I will not say "great, but unnecessary difficulties into the whole "system. These books were universally read "and received by the Jews of our Saviour's time. "He and his Apostles, in common with all other "Jews, referred to them, alluded to them, used "them. Yet, except where he expressly ascribes "a divine authority to particular predictions, I *do* "*not know that we can strictly draw any con-*

"*clusion from the books being so used and applied,*
"*beside the proof,* which it unquestionably is, *of*
"*their notoriety and reception at the time.*"

It will not, I trust, be presumptuous in a Layman if he expresses a hope that, before a bitter controversy about our Lord's sacred person, his divine attributes, and his human nature springs up, Paley's words may be well considered. On the one hand, Bishop Colenso may see ground to reconsider language which seems to impute to the bishops and clergy disbelief in the Church's doctrine, if they do not hold the literal account of the Deluge to be accordant with the facts. On the other hand, those who denounce him as a heretic and a Deist because he has candidly confessed the consequences possibly involved in his inquiries may be induced to modify, or at at least, to suspend their censure; remembering that he spoke of those consequences as opening "questions for reverent criticism," and as pointing to conclusions "consistent," in his opinion, "with the most entire and sincere belief in our "Lord's Divinity."

At any rate, it will not be thought irrelevant to point out to other laymen, that in the opinion of such a man as Paley, "a reference in the New

"Testament to a passage in the Old does not so "fix its authority as to exclude all inquiry into "its credibility, or into the separate reasons upon "which that credibility is founded." It is much to be wished that Bishop Colenso had weighed well the words which follow :—" It is unwarrant- "able, as well as an unsafe rule, to lay down "concerning the Jewish history what was never "laid down concerning any other, that every par- "ticular of it must be true, or the whole false."

III. Let it then be granted that Christians are at liberty, as Paley says, to inquire into "the separate grounds of the credibility" of portions of the Old Testament, and let the particular language unfortunately used by the Bishop of Natal be put aside for the moment, while we ask what, in substance, he has proved or attempted to prove? The principal questions to which he has drawn attention are—

1. The variance between facts on the surface of the globe, now generally known, and the Scriptural accounts of the Creation and Deluge.

2. The authorship and date of some books of the Pentateuch.

(1.) Under the first head, the whole force of his remarks on the unhistorical character of the

Pentateuch is derived from the supposition, that either the literal account of physical details is to be taken as matter of scientific record, revealed by divine authority, or that the account is wholly worthless. No doubt many clergymen do speak as if they so thought. Many earnest workers in science are thereby repelled from the Church, if not from Christianity. With regard to the Deluge, it is now almost certain that there are no traces of an Universal Deluge; but rather that there is positive evidence of the contrary. Hugh Miller has collected the evidence in his 'Testimony of the Rocks.' Any educated man may judge of it. The Bible account of the Flood bears no sign of being poetic; on the other hand, it does not bear the marks of contemporary narrative. May we not, on many grounds, conclude that it is a later account of a great judgment, based on tradition?

Certainly Bishop Colenso has not proved, nor, it is believed, has any geologist shown, that there are well-ascertained facts adverse to a *bonâ fide* deluge *of some kind*, from which Noah and his family were saved. How needless, therefore, has been the Bishop's outbreak about the Baptismal Service! Yet may not what he has said be traced to an overstrained scruple, arising perhaps from excited feeling, produced by his isolated position and by what he considers undeserved treatment?

If we turn to the account of the Creation, we are led to a very different conclusion as to the purport of the record. I will give that conclusion in the words of a candid writer, of whom I know only what he has written in the volume of 'Replies to the Essays and Reviews' published with a preface by the Bishop of Oxford. Mr. Rorison, incumbent of Peterhead, Aberdeen, rejects successively the ideas that the first chapter of Genesis is a "history or narrative," a "myth," a "parable," a "vision," or a "plan." He says, we "venture to think none of these descriptions satis-"factory;" he decides that "the Book of Gene-"sis opens with the inspired PSALM of Creation." A little further on, he says: 'On the hypothesis "that we have to do with an ordinary prose nar-"rative, chronicle, or diary, there immediately "emerges the great difficulty of the 'days.' "With this it is not much to say that no inge-"nuity has as yet grappled successfully. The "choice lies between the Chalmerian interpola-"tion of the geological ages before the first day

"begins, and the Cuvierian expansion of the six
"days into geological ages. For these solutions
"respectively, Dr. Buckland* and Hugh Miller
"have each done their best, and more skilful ad-
"vocacy could not be found." Mr. Rorison rejects both, apparently regarding them as mere
"makeshifts."

Thus we have a candid defender of the veracity of the Bible, selected as the champion of orthodoxy, writing with reverence and great fulness of information, confessing that many of the attempts to evade difficulties are "palpable subterfuges." The account of the Creation is, in his view, a Psalm. The days are not periods of time; they are part of the imagery; the sequence is one, not of time, but of dignity, rising from the material to the spiritual. And how wonderful is its teaching! How does it lay a foundation for all revealed religion; for our knowledge of the supremacy of man over nature, of our individual spiritual life, and of the origin of family life, as our Lord says, "From the begin-
"ning of the Creation God made them male and
"female." (Mark x. 6.)

* The name of Dr. Pusey should be coupled with that of Dr. Buckland.

It is much to be desired that such frank admissions as Mr. Rorison has made should be endorsed by those in authority.

(2.) It was apparently under the impression that there was no middle course open to a clergyman of the Church of England, between a denial or perversion of facts, and a reconsideration of the authority of the ancient records, that Bishop Colenso applied himself to the examination of the credentials of that authority. Into the details of this examination I have no intention of following him. You have done wisely to take ground more suited to us laymen.

But I wish to call the attention of the young friends, for whom I suppose myself to be writing as your lay assessor, to the results of Bishop Colenso's two books—results the importance of which he seems enormously to overrate.

Suppose his facts (those, I mean, which are not simply trifling) be admitted—what is the utmost they prove? On the negative side they cannot prove more than these propositions:—
1st. That the Book of Exodus, as we now have it, is not a contemporary work. 2nd. That there are signs in the Book of Genesis, and in other books, that they were not written by one single

hand. 3rd. He will probably complete the chain by showing, what is held by many critics on the Continent, that the Book of Deuteronomy bears marks of a different hand and of a later date than the other books. Well, what then? In what respect are we likely to be the wiser or the better for these questions being thrust on the attention of the laity in every country town, before their moral and spiritual import has been duly considered and recognized? Such facts, or, at least, such opinions, have long been known on the Continent; they have been kept out of sight in England as Rationalism. Will it make any real difference to us, as Christians, whichever way they shall eventually be settled, if indeed they can be settled?

But let us look at the positive results of the Bishop's writings. On the details of his theory I am not competent to form an opinion. It requires the life of a scholar to decide on such questions. Even Niebuhr was not so sure in constructing as in destroying. But I speak the opinion of one who is able to judge when I say that the Bishop, in his theory about Samuel, has given us nothing but a *"baseless conjecture."* This is the opinion of one who has followed his facts closely, and who had arrived in substance at all that he has really proved long ago.

IV. The Bishop has, it seems to me, entirely confounded two essentially different questions—the authorship of certain books, and the authority of the "Word of God." He may, or he may not, have proved their authorship to be later than was commonly supposed; he has not touched the question of their credibility as history, of their authority, or of their inspiration. But while he has not examined the principles by which such questions must be decided, he has taken on trust, as you have clearly shown, most questionable premises, and drawn his conclusions in a manner which can only be called violent. The Bishop seems to proceed throughout on the assumption, that to prove a book to be incorrect or inconsistent is to prove it uninspired, or, in other words, that an inspired book must be in all things infallible. Many of his opponents seem to accept his terms, and to make the same assumption.

I am not about to offer any opinion of my own on a most difficult subject, namely, inspiration. You have treated it from one point of view; I might be disposed to look at it from another.

I wish only to call attention to the fact that this assumption made by the Bishop and by many of his opponents, is not held by persons whose opinion is entitled to great weight.*

Dean Alford,† speaking of the Gospels, says that "in minor points of accuracy or inaccuracy of "which human research suffices to inform men," such as "conventionally-received distances," "phe-"nomena in natural history, etc.," the "Evange-"lists and Apostles were not supernaturally in-"formed." "The same may be said of citations "and dates from history. In the last apology of "St. Stephen, which he spoke being full of the "Holy Ghost, ... *we have at least two demonstra-*"*ble historical inaccuracies.* And the occurrence "of similar ones in the Gospels *does not in any* "*way affect the inspiration* or the *veracity* of the "Evangelists."

I quote this passage for the importance of the principle, which is quite consistent with another assertion of the learned author, that the inspiration of the sacred writers "enabled them for "their work in a manner which distinguishes

---

* A complete digest or catena of opinions may, as you know, be found in Mr. Stephen's speech in the Court of Arches, published by Smith and Elder.

† Greek Test. vol. i. Prolegom. p. 19, 2nd edition.

"them from all other writers in the world, and "their work from all other works."

The Dean of Ely, to whom I have already referred, has pointed out that no theory of inspiration is given on Divine authority, that none is necessary for the Christian faith, that it is sufficient to maintain that the Bible is the Word of God, without defining how much of fallibility is introduced by its being clothed in human language, nor how far it is consistent with inspiration for the Holy Scriptures to contain "scientific errors," or "historical errors," or "internal discrepancies."

V. I will touch very lightly on the last point, the relation of the present controversy to clerical obligations. I am glad that you have decided not to enter in this publication on any question now under the consideration of the Legislature. I have a very strong feeling that those who are dissatisfied with the present position of affairs in the Universities and in the Church should exhaust every other means of obtaining a remedy at the hands of the constituted authorities before they apply to the House of Commons; so that if any application to Parliament should be necessary, it may be made, if possible, with the weight of united counsels. Perhaps such a hope is visionary.

It is now manifest that the danger lest the Universities and the Church should be weakened by loss of intellectual power is imminent. Into all the causes it is needless now to inquire.

But I may mention that circumstances have brought under my notice the painful position of young and able men who would gladly devote themselves to the cause of education and of the Church. They feel that in order to give a liberal education with full effect, they should have a commission to preach the Gospel to the poor, and to lay down principles for the guidance of the young from the pulpit. But they dare not pledge themselves to an unfeigned belief which may be construed as binding them to exclude from their own minds all fair dealing with critical inquiry.

As far as our Prayer Book is concerned, inpreted as it is by Dr. Lushington's judgment, there would seem little to embarrass a young man who is a sincere Christian, except the fear of the sense which may be put by his Bishop on the Deacon's declaration of unfeigned belief in Holy Scripture.

It would seem that what is most to be desired at the present time, is that some leading mind in authority should make it plain to the young men at the Universities that a declaration of unfeigned belief in Holy Scripture is held, by those who ordain, to be consistent with a progressive recognition of facts which increased investigation may disclose with reference to the Sacred Volume.

The mind of the Church has been clearly declared on the *sufficiency* of Holy Scripture, as containing all things necessary for salvation, after full consideration of the bearings of the Romanist controversy.

But is it not equally clear that the question—whether the Church holds the *infallibility* of the sacred writers with reference to questions raised by modern science and modern criticism—has not yet been decided, because it has not yet been heard before the Church? Dr. Lushington's recent decision, which in part at least is under appeal, declares only the legal and binding effect of existing declarations sanctioned by the Act of Uniformity.

Taking into account the learning, the candour, and personal weight of some of those who compose the Committee recently appointed by Convocation, the Laity may look for their Report with hope, but not without anxiety as to the principles by which they may be guided in their opinion of the publication of the Bishop of Natal.

Yours affectionately,

A Layman.

POSTSCRIPT.

Since this Letter has been in the hands of the printer, I have seen the article on the Bible and the Church in the 'Edinburgh Review;' and, in consequence of the praise there given to a reply to Bishop Colenso's Part I. by a "Layman of the Church of England," published at Skeffington's, I have referred to that volume.

Writing, as I do, on the supposition that your Letters may fall into the hands of many who may not have access to much that is written on this subject, I would venture to advise any one on whom Bishop Colenso's line of argument has had effect to read this book, in order to see how strongly the Bishop can be met on his own ground by an opponent whose courtesy and Christian candour is a model to all who enter into controversy.

I have implied (and I think you agree with me) that Bishop Colenso's mode of reasoning in his book on Exodus is weak and inconclusive, except on certain assumptions, which are needless and unsupported; and that he has been made responsible for conclusions and inferences which he may repudiate.

The answer to which I refer is of great value as narrowing the question. It shows—

1. That Bishop Colenso brings no objections against the probability of revelation, and therefore no objection against miraculous agency, if duly testified.

2. No objections against the Divine element, the spiritual and moral truths of the Bible.

3. That the Bishop accepts the five books as in some sense inspired writings, containing the true Word of God.

4. Further, it shows that Bishop Colenso, in objecting to the historic truth of part of the Bible, does not object to such facts as the Creation, the Fall, the Incarnation, Death, Resurrec-

tion, and Ascension of Christ, as incredible in themselves, but only to another class of historic truths, the objections to which are "vitally different in principle."

The question is thus, as by a skilful pleader, reduced to simplicity of issue.

"Do the statements made in the Pentateuch "about matters which it professes to narrate "as common history contain contradictions and "inconsistencies?" Ay or No? The several counts of the indictment are enumerated under three heads:—

1. Inconsistency with the conditions of the story, and the circumstances of the time set forth in the book itself.

2. Inconsistency between one part of the account and another.

3. Inconsistency with facts otherwise known, such as profane history, geography, etc.

It will be observed that the question of inconsistency with facts of science is not included. The difficulties about the Creation and the Deluge form no part of the "Layman's" argument. I have not yet had time to weigh fully the evidence adduced, but it evidently deserves very careful consideration; and, as against Bishop Colenso's case, it seems to point to the following verdict:—

That a very large proportion of Bishop Colenso's difficulties are of his own making, arising from his having put a meaning on the words of Scripture contrary to common sense; in fact, that the man of straw is put up to be overturned.

That on the more important points he has failed to make out any *demonstrable* impossibility, contradiction, or inconsistency such as would negative the historic truth of the general narrative.

So far negatively. Further, positively. That there is evidence of undesigned coincidences in the actual statements made; and that there are such signs, in the way both of remarkable allusions and of not less remarkable silence, want of method and arrangement, as point to contemporary authorship, at least in many of the details. This conclusion leaves open the question as to the persons by whom, and the time at which, the Pentateuch was reduced to its present form. Of course, it is only by reading and carefully reflecting upon the details of such an argument that any man can do justice to the subject in his own mind if he has allowed weight to the Bishop's details.

It will be a great gain if the work begun by Professor Blunt, of applying the principle of Paley's 'Horæ Paulinæ' to the early books of the Old Testament, be continued, with all the aids of modern criticism, by competent persons, provided that the results be frankly and fairly stated.

Meantime, it may be well to bear in mind, that while the disproof of Bishop Colenso's arithmetical tests of history—supposing it complete—may be for many readers all that they need in order to resettle their minds, such a line of argument will have little or no effect on another class of readers. Therefore, those who speak of the questions raised by the Bishop as disposed of by triumphant refutation are much underrating the work which lies before the guides of religious thought in England.

The "Layman of the Church of England" has stated his own view of the tremendous consequences involved in the inquiry; but, with remarkable candour, he shows that the statement of those consequences has nothing to do with the truth or falsehood of the answer to which inquiry may lead.

He further shows, in a valuable appendix, that the testimony of the New Testament does not prove either the historic character of the Pentateuch or its Mosaic origin; and that it is very unwise to rest the case on that ground.

Therefore, while I think the Church owes a deep debt of gratitude to the "Layman of the Church of England" for the work he has done and for the example he has set, the questions which I originally proposed to you do not the less require answers. Without pledging myself to concurrence with all the opinions expressed in your Letters, I am very grateful for the answers you have given.

Yours affectionately,

A Layman.

NOTE.

It has been suggested that if in the first Letter addressed to Mr. Maurice, page 5, the terms used had been "Science and the Bible" rather than "Science and Revelation," the statement there made would have been less liable to objection. That may be so. But Mr. Maurice's readers will not regret that occasion was given for the letters which he founded on the statement as it stands.

It may not be amiss, however, to add by way of qualification, that it was not intended to deny that there is progress in Revelation, both as regards its manifestation and the capacity of its recipients; nor to deny that in Science there is Revelation to the student who to the requisite diligence adds the patient and child-like spirit of which truly scientific men have offered bright examples.

What was chiefly intended was to assert that if we believe, however that belief be induced, that God does truly reveal Himself in any sense which is above human conceptions and logical rules, then in such belief are involved two admissions. It must be admitted, on the one hand, that the methods of Logical and Natural Science cannot destroy that which is revealed, *so far as it is supernatural*; and if they cannot destroy, they cannot build up. It must be admitted, on the other hand, that the higher knowledge of God, for which Mr. Maurice would most earnestly contend, is not intended to impose fetters on the humble and truthful use of the faculties which God has given us, but rather to set them free, and strengthen them by temperate and orderly use.

To what extent God's revelation or God's Word has been, at any particular time or in any particular manner, supernaturally given (seeing that He has spoken at divers times and in divers manners); how that which is supernatural is connected with that which is natural; what are the several offices of the human reason and conscience, of the written Word, of the Visible Church, and of the Holy Spirit, are questions doubtless closely connected with those addressed for an immediate practical purpose to Mr. Maurice. But they require consideration and reconsideration, and perhaps never required more careful and reverent handling than at this present time.

In the second Letter to Mr. Maurice, all that has any real value is borrowed from a friend, the obligations to whom would be confessed more in detail but for fear of making him answerable for the maimed expressions of his own thoughts.

THE END.

JANUARY, 1868.

16, BEDFORD STREET, COVENT GARDEN,

London.

MACMILLAN AND CO.'S
THEOLOGICAL WORKS.

Bernard.—The Progress of Doctrine in the New Testament. In Eight Lectures preached before the University of Oxford. By THOMAS D. BERNARD, M.A., Rector of Walcot. *Second Edition.* 8vo. 8s. 6d.

Birks.—The Difficulties of Belief in connexion with the Creation and the Fall. By T. R. BIRKS, M.A., Perpetual Curate of Holy Trinity, Cambridge. Crown 8vo. 4s. 6d.

Burgon.—A Treatise on the Pastoral Office. Addressed chiefly to Candidates for Holy Orders, or to those who have recently undertaken the cure of souls. By the Rev. JOHN W. BURGON, M.A., Oxford. 8vo. 12s.

"The spirit in which it approaches and solves practical questions is at once full of common sense and at the same time marked by a deep reverential piety and a largeness of charity which are truly admirable."—*Spectator.*

Butler.—Works by the Rev. WM. ARCHER BUTLER, M.A., late Professor of Moral Philosophy in the University of Dublin:—

— Sermons, Doctrinal and Practical. Edited, with a Memoir of the Author's Life, by T. WOODWARD, M.A., Dean of Down. With Portrait. *Seventh Edition.* 8vo. 8s.

"Present a richer combination of the qualities for Sermons of the first class than any we have met with in any living writer."—*British Quarterly.*

— A Second Series of Sermons. Edited by J. A. JEREMIE, D.D., Regius Professor of Divinity in the University of Cambridge. *Fifth Edition.* 8vo. 7s.

"They are marked by the same originality and vigour of expression, the same richness of imagery and illustration, the same large views and catholic spirit, and the same depth and fervour of devotional feeling, which so remarkably distinguished the preceding Series, and which rendered it a most valuable accession to our theological literature."—*From Dr. Jeremie's Preface.*

— Letters on Romanism, in Reply to Mr. Newman's Essay on Development. Edited by T. WOODWARD, M.A., Dean of Down. 8vo. 10s. 6d.

Butler (G).—Sermons preached in Cheltenham College Chapel. By the Rev. GEO. BUTLER, M.A., Principal of Liverpool College. Crown 8vo. 7s. 6d.

"We can give them high praise for devoutness, soundness, and perspicuity...... The whole volume deserves high commendation."—*Literary Churchman.*

Butler (G).—Family Prayers.
By the Rev. GEO. BUTLER, M.A. Crown 8vo. 5s.
"They are very good, earnest, and Scriptural."—*Literary Churchman.*

Butler (M).—Sermons preached in the Chapel of
Harrow School. By H. MONTAGUE BUTLER, Head Master. Crown 8vo. 7s. 6d.
"We have never read any collection of sermons to young people with more unmingled pleasure than this volume has afforded us. The discourses are in the best sense Scriptural and evangelical; overflowing with Biblical knowledge, and pervaded everywhere by the spirit of the Gospel."—*Freeman.*
"These Sermons are adapted for every Christian household. There is nothing more striking than the excellent good sense with which they are imbued."—*Spectator.*

Calderwood.—Philosophy of the Infinite.
A Treatise on Man's Knowledge of the Infinite Being, in answer to Sir W. Hamilton and Dr. Mansel. By the Rev. HENRY CALDERWOOD, M.A. *Second Edition.* 8vo. 14s.
"A book of great ability . . . . . . written in a clear style and may be easily understood by even those who are not versed in such discussions."—*British Quarterly Review.*
"The Volume is a valuable contribution to what we may term sacred philosophy, full of valuable suggestions, and pervaded everywhere by a warm piety."—*Journal of Sacred Literature.*
"A philosophical and calmly written volume, which ventilates the subject on that positive side of it, upon which we hold Mr. Mansel to have insufficiently dwelt."—*Guardian.*

Cambridge Lent Sermons.—Sermons preached
during Lent, 1864, in Great St. Mary's Church, Cambridge. By the BISHOP of OXFORD, Rev. H. P. LIDDON, T. L. CLAUGHTON, J. R. WOODFORD, Dr. GOULBURN, J. W. BURGON, T. T. CARTER, Dr. PUSEY, DEAN HOOK, W. J. BUTLER, DEAN GOODWIN. Crown 8vo. 7s. 6d.

Campbell.—The Nature of the Atonement and its
Relation to Remission of Sins and Eternal Life. By JOHN M'LEOD CAMPBELL. *Second Edition, revised.* 8vo. 10s. 6d.
"This is a remarkable book, as indicating the mode in which a devout and intellectual mind has found its way, almost unassisted, out of the extreme Lutheran and Calvinistic views of the Atonement into a healthier atmosphere of doctrine . . . . . We cannot assent to all the positions laid down by this writer, but he is entitled to be spoken respectfully of, both because of his evident earnestness and reality, and the tender mode in which he deals with the opinions of others from whom he feels compelled to differ."—*Literary Churchman.*

—— **Thoughts on Revelation, with special reference to the Present Time.** By JOHN M'LEOD CAMPBELL. Crown 8vo. 5s.
"It is rarely that we have to do with a book so original, so profound, and so satisfactory as this little Volume . . . . . developed with admirable force and perspicuity, as well as with a grave and earnest eloquence most becoming such a theme."—*Freeman.*
"The whole of the work is deep and admirable."—*Spectator.*

THEOLOGICAL WORKS.

Chretien.—The Letter and the Spirit.
Six Sermons on the Inspiration of Holy Scripture. By CHARLES P. CHRETIEN. Crown 8vo. 5s.

Clark.—Four Sermons preached in the Chapel of Trinity College, Cambridge. By W. G. CLARK, M.A., Public Orator in the University of Cambridge. Fcap. 8vo. 2s. 6d.

"It is very rare and very refreshing to find so much hard thought and so much clear knowledge exhibited in the compass of a sermon. The sermon on 'General Revelation' strikes us as being a thoughtful piece of theology calculated to be very useful to many minds at the present day."—*Literary Gazette.*

Clay.—The Power of the Keys.
Sermons preached in Coventry. By the Rev. W. L. CLAY, M.A. Fcap. 8vo. 3s. 6d.

Colenso.—Works by the Right Rev. J. W. COLENSO, D.D., Bishop of Natal:—

— Village Sermons.
Seventh Edition. Fcap. 8vo. 2s. 6d.

— Companion to the Holy Communion.
Containing the Service, and Select Readings from the writings of Mr. MAURICE. *Fine Edition,* morocco, antique style, 6s.; or in cloth, 2s. 6d. *Common Paper,* 1s.

— St. Paul's Epistles to the Romans.
Newly Translated and Explained, from a Missionary point of View. Crown 8vo. 7s. 6d.

Cotton.—Works by the late GEORGE EDWARD LYNCH COTTON, D.D., Bishop of Calcutta:—

— Sermons, chiefly connected with Public Events of 1854. Fcap. 8vo. 3s.

— Expository Sermons on the Epistles for the Sundays of the Christian Year. Two Vols. Crown 8vo. 15s.

"May be best described by ranking them with the similar, and of their kind excellent, productions of Dr. Vaughan. They are the work of an independent thinker and good scholar."—*Guardian.*

— Sermons preached to English Congregations in India. Crown 8vo. 7s. 6d.

"They are as the editor says, 'calm, persuasive teachings,' but they are marked by fidelity to evangelical truth, by an attractive catholicity of feeling, and by a fresh, simple, practical earnestness of purpose, which give them a great charm."—*British Quarterly Review.*

"The Sermons are models of what sermons should be, not only on account of their practical teaching, but also with regard to the singular felicity with which they are adapted to times, places, and circumstances."—*Spectator.*

Clergyman's Self-Examination concerning the Apostles' Creed. Extra fcap. 8vo. 1s. 6d.

Davies.—Works by the Rev. J. LL. DAVIES, M.A., Rector of Christ Church, St. Marylebone.

— **The Work of Christ;** or the World Reconciled to God. With a Preface on the Atonement Controversy. Fcap. 8vo. 6s.

— **Sermons on the Manifestation of the Son of God.** With a Preface addressed to Laymen on the present position of the Clergy of the Church of England; and an Appendix on the Testimony of Scripture and the Church as to the possibility of Pardon in the Future State. Fcap. 8vo. 6s. 6d.

— **Baptism, Confirmation, and the Lord's Supper,** as interpreted by their Outward Signs. Three Expository Addresses for Parochial use. Limp cloth, 1s. 6d.

— **The Epistles of St. Paul to the Ephesians, the Colossians, and Philemon.** With Introductions and Notes, and an Essay on the Traces of Foreign Elements in the Theology of these Epistles. 8vo. 7s. 6d.

— **Morality according to the Sacrament of the Lord's Supper.** Crown 8vo. 3s. 6d.

"Of this school of Christian theology Mr. Davies is one of the most accomplished and able teachers, and in these fine Sermons, preached before the University of Cambridge, on the Divine morality of the Lord's Supper, he has done much to strike both at the error of the mystic ritualism which founds the Lord's Supper on a hypothetical physical miracle, which, even were it true, would give no additional sacredness to the spiritual meaning of the Service, and also at the error of the empty rationalism which, regarding the whole Service as ceremonial, and therefore totally distinct from the highest morality, despises it altogether."—*Spectator.*

De Teissier.—Works by G. F. DE TEISSIER, B.D.:

— **Village Sermons.** Crown 8vo. 9s.

— **Second Series.** Crown 8vo. 8s. 6d.

— **The House of Prayer;** or, a Practical Exposition of the Order for Morning and Evening Prayer in the Church of England. 18mo. extra cloth, 4s. 6d.

"The work of an able and scholarlike mind..... Their tone, both of doctrine and exhortation is thoroughly sound and practical."—*Guardian.*
"Eminently practical and penetrating, and pregnant with thought......... uniformly good throughout; these Sermons not unfrequently remind us of the Parochial Sermons of J. H. Newman."—*Literary Churchman.*

Donaldson.—A Critical History of Christian Literature and Doctrine, from the Death of the Apostles to the Nicene Council. By JAMES DONALDSON, LL.D. 3 vols. 8vo. cloth, 31s. 6d.

Ecce Homo.—A Survey of the Life and Work of Jesus Christ. *Eighth Edition.* Crown 8vo. 6s.

Theological Works.

Forbes.—Village Sermons by a Northamptonshire Rector. With a Preface on the Inspiration of Holy Scripture. Crown 8vo. 6s.

"Such a volume as the present, which seems to us to preach the pure essence of Christ's Gospel in the simplest language, and yet with a warmth and force that cannot fail to drive it home to men cultured or uncultured alike. . . . . is as great an accession to the cause of a deep theology as the most refined exposition of its fundamental principle."—*Spectator.*

— The Voice of God in the Psalms.
By GRANVILLE FORBES, Rector of Broughton. Crown 8vo. 6s. 6d.

"Sermons of a superior class, both as to material, as to their mutual connexion and sequence of thought, and as to expression."—*Literary Churchman.*

Gifford.—The Glory of God in Man.
By E. H. GIFFORD, D.D. Fcap. 8vo. cloth, 3s. 6d.

Hardwick.—Works by the Ven. ARCHDEACON HARDWICK:—

— Christ and other Masters.
A Historical Inquiry into some of the Chief Parallelisms and Contrasts between Christianity and the Religious Systems of the Ancient World. *New Edition,* revised, and a Prefatory Memoir by the Rev. FRANCIS PROCTER. Two vols. crown 8vo. 15s.

— A History of the Christian Church.
MIDDLE AGE. From Gregory the Great to the Excommunication of Luther. Edited by FRANCIS PROCTER, M.A. With Four Maps constructed for this work by A. KEITH JOHNSTON. *Second Edition.* Crown 8vo. 10s. 6d.

— A History of the Christian Church during the REFORMATION. Revised by FRANCIS PROCTER, M.A. *Second Edition.* Crown 8vo. 10s. 6d.

— Twenty Sermons for Town Congregations.
Crown 8vo. 6s. 6d.

Hervey.—The Genealogies of our Lord and Saviour Jesus Christ, as contained in the Gospels of St. Matthew and St. Luke, reconciled with each other, and shown to be in harmony with the true Chronology of the Times. By Lord ARTHUR HERVEY, M.A. 8vo. 10s. 6d.

Howard.—The Pentateuch; or, the Five Books of Moses. Translated into English from the Version of the LXX. With Notes on its Omissions and Insertions, and also on the Passages in which it differs from the Authorized Version. By the Hon. HENRY HOWARD, D.D., Dean of Lichfield. Crown 8vo. GENESIS, 1 vol. 8s. 6d.; EXODUS and LEVITICUS, 1 vol. 10s. 6d.; NUMBERS and DEUTERONOMY, 1 vol. 10s. 6d.

Hymni Ecclesiæ.—Fcap. 8vo. cloth. 7s. 6d.

Jones.—The Church of England and Common Sense. By HARRY JONES, M.A. Fcap. 8vo. cloth, 3s. 6d.

Kingsley.—Works by the Rev. CHARLES KINGSLEY, M.A., Rector of Eversley, and Professor of Modern History in the University of Cambridge:—

— Good News of God.
Fourth Edition. Fcap. 8vo. 4s. 6d.

— Village Sermons.
Seventh Edition. Fcap. 8vo. 2s. 6d.

— Town and Country Sermons.
Fcap. 8vo. 6s.

— The Gospel of the Pentateuch.
Second Edition. Fcap. 8vo. 4s. 6d.

— Sermons for the Times.
Third Edition. Fcap. 8vo. 3s. 6d.

— DAVID. Four Sermons.
David's Weakness—David's Strength—David's Anger—David's Deserts. Fcap. 8vo. 2s. 6d.

— Sermons on National Subjects.
First Series. *Second Edition.* Fcap. 8vo. 5s.

— Sermons on National Subjects.
Second Series. *Second Edition.* Fcap. 8vo. 5s.

— The Water of Life, and other Sermons.
Fcap. 8vo. 6s.

— Discipline, and other Sermons.   [*In the Press.*

Maclaren.—Sermons preached at Manchester.
By ALEXANDER MACLAREN. *Second Edition.* Fcp. 8vo. 4s. 6d. *A Second Series in the Press.*
"The Sermons are clear and original."—*Guardian.*
"It is quite refreshing to find a volume so full, thoughtful, elegant, and yet at the same time so sound and so thoroughly practical as this is."—*Record.*

Mackenzie.—The Christian Clergy of the First Ten Centuries, and their Influence on European Civilization. By HENRY MACKENZIE, B.A., Scholar of Trinity College, Cambridge. Crown 8vo. 6s. 6d.

M'Cosh.—Works by JAMES M'COSH, LL.D., Professor of Logic and Metaphysics, Queen's College, Belfast, &c.:—

M'Cosh.—The Method of the Divine Government,
Physical and Moral. *Ninth Edition.* 8vo. 10s. 6d.

— The Supernatural in relation to the Natural.
Crown 8vo. 7s. 6d.

— The Intuitions of the Mind.
A New Edition. 8vo. cloth, 10s. 6d.

"Dr. M'Cosh is worthy of deliberate attention."—*Athenæum.*
"The work of Dr. M'Cosh stands on as high Christian grounds as can well be occupied, and may be regarded as a large instalment towards that thorough Christian philosophy of mind which has so long been a desideratum."—*Literary Churchman.*

Maclear.—Works by G. F. MACLEAR, B.D., Head Master of King's College School, and Preacher at the Temple Church :—

— A History of Christian Missions during the Middle Ages. Crown 8vo. 10s. 6d.

"We gladly welcome the book itself, as bringing within the reach of ordinary readers a portion of Church history full of instruction, yet commonly either unknown or (until late) contemptuously ignored; and as accomplishing this task by a fairly thorough use of both trustworthy modern writers, and the original authorities themselves...... His book is a concise, impartial, thoughtful abridgement of a large subject presented in as attractive a way as such conditions will admit, drawn from good sources, and written with thorough good taste and feeling."—*Guardian.*

— The Witness of the Eucharist; or, The Institution and Early Celebration of the Lord's Supper, considered as an Evidence of the Historical Truth of the Gospel Narrative and of the Atonement. Crown 8vo. 4s. 6d.

Marriner.—Sermons preached at Lyme Regis.
By E. T. MARRINER, Curate. Fcap. 8vo. 4s. 6d.

"All are characterised by great freshness and frequent brilliancy. On the whole the volume is a good specimen of the most interesting and useful kind of preaching now to be heard in the Church of England."—*Freeman.*

Maurice.—Works by the Rev. FREDERICK DENISON MAURICE, M.A., Professor of Moral Philosophy in the University of Cambridge:—

— The Claims of the Bible and of Science; a Correspondence on some questions respecting the Pentateuch. Crown 8vo. 4s. 6d.

— Dialogues on Family Worship.
Crown 8vo. 6s.

— The Patriarchs and Lawgivers of the Old Testament. *Third and Cheaper Edition.* Crown 8vo. 5s.

This volume contains Discourses on the Pentateuch, Joshua, Judges, and the beginning of the First Book of Samuel.

Maurice.—The Prophets and Kings of the Old Testament. *Second Edition.* Crown 8vo. 10s. 6d.

This volume contains Discourses on Samuel I. and II., Kings I. and II., Amos, Joel, Hosea, Isaiah, Micah, Nahum, Habakkuk, Jeremiah, and Ezekiel.

— The Gospel of the Kingdom of Heaven.
A Series of Lectures on the Gospel of St. Luke. Crown 8vo. 9s.

— The Gospel of St. John: a Series of Discourses. *Third and Cheaper Edition.* Crown 8vo. 6s.

— The Epistles of St. John: a Series of Lectures on Christian Ethics. *Second and Cheaper Edition.* Crown 8vo. 6s.

— The Commandments considered as Instruments of National Reformation. Crown 8vo. 4s. 6d.

— Expository Sermons on the Prayer-Book. The Prayer-Book considered especially in reference to the Romish System. *Second Edition.* Fcap. 8vo. 5s. 6d.

— Lectures on the Apocalypse; or, Book of the Revelation of St. John the Divine. Crown 8vo. 10s. 6d.

— What is Revelation? A Series of Sermons on the Epiphany, to which are added Letters to a Theological Student on the Bampton Lectures of Mr. MANSEL. Crown 8vo. 10s. 6d.

— Sequel to the Inquiry, "What is Revelation?" Letters in Reply to Mr. Mansel's Examination of "Strictures on the Bampton Lectures." Crown 8vo. 6s.

— Lectures on Ecclesiastical History.
8vo. 10s. 6d.

— Theological Essays.
Second Edition. Crown 8vo. 10s. 6d.

— The Doctrine of Sacrifice Deduced from the Scriptures. Crown 8vo. 7s. 6d.

— The Religions of the World, and their Relations to Christianity. *Fourth Edition.* Fcap. 8vo. 5s.

— On the Lord's Prayer.
Fourth Edition. Fcap. 8vo. 2s. 6d.

— On the Sabbath Day: the Character of the Warrior; and on the Interpretation of History. Fcap. 8vo. 2s. 6d.

— Learning and Working. Six Lectures on the Foundation of Colleges for Working Men. Crown 8vo. 5s.

Theological Works. 9

Moorhouse.—Some Modern Difficulties respecting the Facts of Nature and Revelation. By JAMES MOORHOUSE, M.A., Perpetual Curate of Paddington, Middlesex. Fcap. 8vo. 2s. 6d.

— Our Lord Jesus Christ the subject of Growth in Wisdom. Four Sermons (being the Hulsean Lectures for 1865) preached before the University of Cambridge; to which is added Three Sermons preached before the University of Cambridge in February 1864. By JAMES MOORHOUSE, M.A. Crown 8vo. 5s.

"He reasons ably and profoundly upon the deep mysteries involved in the subject, and abstains, we think, with sufficient care from pressing human reasoning on such a subject too far. The three Sermons also appended to the volume are suggestive and thoughtful."—*Guardian.*

"Few more valuable works have come into our hands for many years...... a most fruitful and welcome volume."—*Church Review.*

Morse.—Working for God, and other Practical Sermons. By FRANCIS MORSE, M.A. *Second Edition.* Fcap. 8vo. 5s.

Naville.—The Heavenly Father.

By ERNEST NAVILLE, Corresponding Member of the Institute of France, and formerly Professor of Philosophy in the University of Geneva. Translated by HENRY DOWNTON, M.A., English Chaplain at Geneva. Extra fcap. 8vo. 7s. 6d.

"We are happy to hear that Professor Ernest Naville's admirable lectures on infidelity, entitled *"Le Père Celeste,"* which we lately reviewed, has been translated into the Russian, Dutch, modern Greek, and the Moldavian languages, as well as into German and Italian. We trust that the Rev. Mr. Downton's admirable English Translation will have a wide circulation in this country. It would almost seem as if the distinguished lecturer had written purposely for the benefit of England, and to expose the folly of the new importations of Continental atheism....... For depth of thought and lucid comprehension of his subject, as well as for condensation of eloquence, Professor Naville has few competitors."—*Record.*

"This is a work of no common kind. Even if the name of the distinguished author had not appeared on the titlepage, no intelligent reader could have perused a page of the volume without perceiving that it was the production of a richly cultivated and masculine mind in alliance with the highest order of reasoning powers."—*Morning Advertiser.*

O'Brien.—Works by JAMES THOMAS O'BRIEN, D.D., Bishop of Ossory:—

— An Attempt to Explain and Establish the Doctrine of Justification by Faith only. *Third Edition.* 8vo. 12s

"There are few students of Holy Scripture who will not accept it with satisfaction and gratitude ...... we have risen from its perusal with a high degree of pleasure and satisfaction."—*London Quarterly Review.*

— Charge delivered at the Visitation in 1863. *Second Edition.* 8vo. 2s.

— Vindication of the Irish Clergy. 8vo. 2s. 6d.

— Charge delivered in 1866. 8vo. 2s.

Plea for a New English Version of the Scriptures.
By a LICENTIATE of the Church of Scotland. 8vo. 6s.

Potter.—A Voice from the Church in Australia:
Sermons preached in Melbourne. By the Rev. ROBERT POTTER, M.A. Extra fcap. 8vo. 4s. 6d.

Procter.—A History of the Book of Common Prayer: with a Rationale of its Offices. By FRANCIS PROCTER, M.A. *Sixth Edition*, revised and enlarged. Crn. 8vo. 10s. 6d.

> In the course of the last twenty years the whole question of liturgical knowledge has been reopened with great learning and accurate research, and it is mainly with the view of epitomizing their extensive publications, and correcting by their help the errors and misconceptions which had obtained currency, that the present volume has been put together.

Psalms, The, Chronologically Arranged.
An Amended Version, with Historical Introductions and Explanatory Notes. By FOUR FRIENDS. Cr. 8vo. cl. 10s. 6d.

Rays of Sunlight for Dark Days.
A Book of Selections for the Suffering. With a Preface by C. J. VAUGHAN, D.D. 18mo. *New Edition*. 3s. 6d.; morocco, old style, 7s. 6d.

Reynolds.—Notes of the Christian Life.
A Selection of Sermons by HENRY ROBERT REYNOLDS, B.A., President of Cheshunt College, and Fellow of University College, London. Crown 8vo. 7s. 6d.

> "Thorough scholarship and refined taste, whose sermons are not theological disquisitions, but extremely careful and discriminating exhibitions of different phases of Christian experience, and earnest appeals to the heart and conscience on great points of Christian duty. . . . . The reader throughout feels himself in the grasp of an earnest and careful thinker."—*Patriot*.

Roberts.—Discussions on the Gospels.
By the Rev. ALEXANDER ROBERTS, D.D. *Second Edition*, revised and enlarged. 8vo. 16s.

> "It is only bare justice to Dr. Roberts to bear unqualified testimony to the scholarlike fairness and completeness with which he handles the subject."—*Guardian*.

Robertson.—Pastoral Counsels. Being Chapters on Practical and Devotional Subjects. By the Rev. JOHN ROBERTSON, D.D. *Third Edition*, with a Preface by the Author of "The Recreations of a Country Parson." Extra fcap. 8vo. 6s.

Romanis.—Sermons preached at St. Mary's, Reading.
By WILLIAM ROMANIS, M.A. *First Series*. Fcap. 8vo. 6s.

> "Distinguished by accuracy of thought and clearness of expression."—*English Churchman*.

— **Second Series.** Fcap. 8vo. 6s.

Theological Works.

Scott.—Discourses.
By ALEXANDER J. SCOTT, M.A., Professor of Logic in Owen's College, Manchester. Crown 8vo. 7s. 6d.
"The work of no common thinker."—*Literary Churchman.*
"Professor Scott's many friends and admirers will gladly receive as a memorial of his remarkable powers these interesting literary remains...... They are full of fine and high thoughts; calculated to inspire like thoughts in all readers capable of such thinking."—*Scotsman.*

Selwyn.—The Work of Christ in the World.
By G. A. SELWYN, D.D. *Third Edition.* Crown 8vo. 2s.

— **Verbal Analysis of the Bible.**
Folio. 14s.

Sergeant.—Sermons.
By the Rev. E. W. SERGEANT, M.A., Assistant Master at Winchester College. Fcap. 8vo. 2s. 6d.

Shirley.—Elijah; Four University Sermons.
I. Samaria.—II. Carmel.—III. Kishon.—IV. Horeb. By W. W. SHIRLEY, D.D., Professor of Ecclesiastical History in the University of Oxford. Fcap. 8vo. 2s. 6d.
"These Sermons indicate ability of a high order in the cause of sound theology and practical religion."—*Record.*
"The character and times of Elijah are ably pourtrayed in the four sermons before us, and a forcible analogy is instituted by Professor Shirley between the trials and troubles of the prophet's day and our own."—*Literary Churchman.*

Simpson.—An Epitome of the History of the Christian Church. By WILLIAM SIMPSON, M.A. *Fourth Edition.* Fcap. 8vo. 3s. 6d.

Swainson.—Works by C. A. Swainson, D.D., Norrisian Professor of Divinity at Cambridge:—

— **A Handbook to Butler's Analogy.**
Crown 8vo. 1s. 6d.

— **The Creeds of the Church in their Relations to** Holy Scripture and the Conscience of the Christian. 8vo. 9s.

— **The Authority of the New Testament, and** other Lectures, delivered before the University of Cambridge. 8vo. 12s.

Taylor.—The Restoration of Belief.
New and Revised Edition. By ISAAC TAYLOR, Esq. Crown 8vo. 8s. 6d.
"The current of thoughts which runs through this book is calm and clear, its tone is earnest, its manner courteous. The author has carefully studied the successive problems which he so ably handles, and we feel as we read, that he at least understands the workings of unbelief, while he is under the power of faith."—*Journal of Sacred Literature.*

Temple.—Sermons Preached in Rugby School Chapel in 1858, 1859, 1860. By FREDERICK TEMPLE, D.D., Chaplain in Ordinary to her Majesty, Head Master of Rugby School, Chaplain to the Right Hon. the Earl of Denbigh. *New and Cheaper Edition.* Crown 8vo. 7s. 6d.

Thring.—Sermons delivered at Uppingham School. By the Rev. E. THRING, M.A., Head Master. Crown 8vo. 5s.

Thrupp.—Works by the Rev. J. F. THRUPP :—

— Introduction to the Study and use of the Psalms. 2 vols. 8vo. 21s.

"Mr. Thrupp's learned, sound, and sensible work fills a gap hitherto unfilled by any of its predecessors. The book deserves to be strongly recommended to all students, not the learned only, but all educated persons who desire to understand soundly the literal, and so to be able to realize intelligently the typical or prophetical meanings of the Psalter. It is the work of a painstaking and careful Hebrew scholar, of a sound English divine, and of an interpreter singularly fair and straightforward. We end by heartily commending the book to all intelligent students of a portion of the Bible, more often read, but very commonly less understood than others, and which in private reading is much more frequently than it should be the subject of an unintelligent devotion."—*Guardian.*

"Gives evidence not only of a well-read student in the labours of others, but of a reverent, and at the same time independent habit of thought."—*Christian Remembrancer.*

— The Song of Songs. A New Translation, with a Commentary and an Introduction. Crown 8vo. 7s. 6d.

"Of the general features of this work we may briefly say, that it has its foundation laid in sound learning and good sense; that it manifests much acuteness in the perception of slight and half hidden indications of purpose and in the combinations of minute circumstances into a probable and mutually illustrative group: that it is marked by deepest reverence for even the words of Scripture, and has a pervading Scriptural tone and lively feeling; and that it is written with the most perfect clearness, and an elegance which one hardly expects in such a work, but which greatly adds to its enjoyableness."—*Nonconformist.*

"It will give unfeigned satisfaction to those who deeply value the Bible, especially in these evil times, to find a learned and reverent scholar like Mr. Thrupp bestowing his labours upon the commonly neglected and unread Book of Scripture...... We have to express a hearty satisfaction in his revival of the Patristic interpretation of the Song."—*Guardian.*

Todd.—The Books of the Vaudois. The Waldensian Manuscripts preserved in the Library of Trinity College, Dublin, with an Appendix by JAMES HENTHORN TODD, D.D., Professor of Hebrew at Dublin University. Crown 8vo. 6s.

Tracts for Priests and People. By Various Writers. First and Second Series. Crown 8vo. 8s. each.

— Nos. one to fifteen, sewed. 1s. each.

Theological Works.

Trench.—Works by R. CHENEVIX TRENCH, D.D., Archbishop of Dublin:—

— Notes on the Parables of our Lord.
   Tenth Edition. 8vo. 12s.

— Notes on the Miracles of our Lord.
   Eighth Edition. 8vo. 12s.

— Sermons preached in Westminster Abbey.
   Second Edition. 8vo. 10s. 6d.

— On the Authorized Version of the New Testament. Second Edition. 7s.

— Commentary on the Epistles to the Seven Churches in Asia. Third Edition, revised. 8s. 6d.

— Synonyms of the New Testament.
   New Edition. 1 vol. 8vo. 10s. 6d.

— The Fitness of Holy Scripture for Unfolding the Spiritual Life of Man; Christ the Desire of all Nations; or the Unconscious Prophecies of Heathendom. Hulsean Lectures, Fcap. 8vo. Fourth Edition. 5s.

— Subjection of the Creature to Vanity, and other Sermons. Fcap. 8vo. 3s.

— Studies in the Gospels.
   Second Edition. 8vo. 10s. 6d.

— Shipwrecks of Faith: Three Sermons preached before the University of Cambridge, in May, 1867. Fcap. 8vo. 2s. 6d.

— Primary Charge.
   8vo. 2s.

— Charge delivered in 1866.
   8vo. 1s.

— Brief Notes on the Greek of the New Testament (for English Readers). By the Rev. FRANCIS TRENCH, M.A. Crown 8vo. cloth. 6s.
   "A very useful work, enabling the unlearned reader to see at once the places in which our translation is not quite literal or defective in force."—*Spectator*.

— Four Assize Sermons, preached at York and Leeds. By the Rev. FRANCIS TRENCH, M.A. Crown 8vo. cloth, 2s. 6d.

Tudor.—**The Decalogue Viewed as the Christian's Law,** with special reference to the Questions and Wants of the Times. By the Rev. RICHARD TUDOR, B.A. Crown 8vo. 10s. 6d.

"Mr. Tudor writes earnestly and reverently, and he has not shrunk from dealing with very difficult and thorny questions, such as the unity of the Church, the Commination Service, the Athanasian Creed, the Sabbath, Suicide, War, Divorce, the Prohibited Degrees of Marriage, Equivocation, Simony. The volume constitutes a thoughtful application of the principles involved in the Ten Commandments to the circumstances of the present day."—*Christian Remembrancer.*

Tulloch.—**The Christ of the Gospels and the Christ of Modern Criticism.** Lectures on M. RENAN's "Vie de Jésus." By JOHN TULLOCH, D.D., Principal of the College of St. Mary, in the University of St. Andrew. Extra fcap. 8vo. 4s. 6d.

"Amongst direct answers to M. Renan this volume will not be easily surpassed: the style is animated, pointed and scholarly; the tone fair and appreciative; the philosophy intelligent and cautious; the Christianity reverent and hearty. Dr. Tulloch's book is sure to be widely read, and may be recommended without reserve for popular reading."—*The Reader.*

Vaughan.—Works by CHARLES J. VAUGHAN, D.D., Vicar of Doncaster:—

— **Memorials of Harrow Sundays.**
A Selection of Sermons preached in Harrow School Chapel. With a View of the Chapel. *Fourth Edition.* Crown 8vo. 10s. 6d.

— **St. Paul's Epistle to the Romans.**
The Greek Text with English Notes. *New Edition.*
[*In the Press.*

— **Revision of the Liturgy.**
Twelve Discourses on Liturgical Subjects. Fcap. 8vo. 6s.

— **Epiphany, Lent, and Easter.**
A Selection of Expository Sermons. *Second Edition.* Crown 8vo. 10s. 6d.

— **Lectures on the Epistle to the Philippians.**
Second Edition. Crown 8vo. 7s. 6d.

— **The Book and the Life: and other Sermons,**
Preached before the University of Cambridge. *New Edition.* Fcap. 8vo. 4s. 6d.

— **Lectures on the Revelation of St. John.**
Second Edition. 2 vols. crown 8vo. 15s.

— **Lessons of Life and Godliness.**
A Selection of Sermons preached in the Parish Church of Doncaster. *Third Edition.* Fcap. 8vo. 4s. 6d.

Vaughan (C. J).—Words from the Gospels.
A Second Selection of Sermons preached in the Parish Church of Doncaster. *Second Edition.* Fcap. 8vo. 4s. 6d.

— The Epistles of St. Paul.
For English Readers. Part I. containing the First Epistle to the Thessalonians. *Second Edition.* 8vo. 1s. 6d. (Each Epistle will be published separately.)

— The Church of the First Days:
Series I. The Church of Jerusalem. *Second Edition.*
   " II. The Church of the Gentiles. *Second Edition.*
   " III. The Church of the World. *Second Edition.*
Fcap. 8vo. 4s. 6d. each.

— The Wholesome Words of Jesus Christ.
Four Sermons preached before the University of Cambridge, in November, 1866. Fcap. 8vo. 3s. 6d.

Vaughan.—Works by DAVID J. VAUGHAN, M.A., Vicar of St. Martin's, Leicester:—

— Sermons preached in St. John's Church, Leicester, during the Years 1855 and 1856. Crown 8vo. 5s. 6d.

— Sermons on the Resurrection. With a Preface.
Fcap. 8vo. 3s.

— Christian Evidences and the Bible.
New Edition, revised and enlarged. Fcap. 8vo. cloth, 5s. 6d.
"This little volume is a model of that honest and reverent criticism of the Bible which it is not only right but the duty of English clergymen in such times as these to put forth from the pulpit."—*The Spectator.*

— Sermons on Sacrifice and Propitiation.
Fcap. 8vo. 2s. 6d.

Westcott.—Works by BROOKE FOSS WESTCOTT, B.D., Assistant Master in Harrow School:—

— A General Survey of the History of the Canon of the New Testament during the First Four Centuries. Crown 8vo. *Second Edition.* Revised. 10s. 6d.

— Characteristics of the Gospel Miracles.
Sermons preached before the University of Cambridge. *With Notes.* Crown 8vo. 4s. 6d.

— Introduction to the Study of the Four Gospels.
Third Edition. Crown 8vo. 10s. 6d.

— The Bible in the Church.
A Popular Account of the Collection and Reception of the Holy Scriptures in the Christian Churches. *Second Edition.* 18mo. 4s. 6d.

Westcott.—The Gospel of the Resurrection:
Thoughts on its Relation to Reason and History. *New Edition.* Fcap. 8vo. 4s. 6d.

Wilson.—An English Hebrew and Chaldee Lexicon
and Concordance to the more correct understanding of the English Translation of the Old Testament, by reference to the Original Hebrew. By WILLIAM WILSON, D.D., Canon of Winchester, late Fellow of Queens' College, Oxford. *Second Edition*, carefully revised. 4to. cloth, 25s.

Wilton.—The Negeb; or, "South Country" of
Scripture. By the Rev. EDWARD WILTON, M.A., Oxon. With a Map. Crown 8vo. 7s. 6d.

Witt.—The Mutual Influence of the Christian
Doctrine and the School of Alexandria. By J. G. WITT, B.A. (The Hulsean Prize Essay for 1860.) Crown 8vo. 2s. 6d.

Woodford.—Christian Sanctity.
By J. RUSSELL WOODFORD, M.A. Fcap. 8vo. cloth. 3s.

Woodward.—Works by the Rev. HENRY WOODWARD, M.A. Edited by his Son, THOMAS WOODWARD, M.A., Dean of Down:—

— The Shunammite.
Second Edition. Crown 8vo. cloth. 10s. 6d.

— Sermons.
Fifth Edition. Crown 8vo. 10s. 6d.

Worship (The) of God and Fellowship among Men.
Sermons on Public Worship. By Professor MAURICE and Others. Fcap. 8vo. cloth. 3s. 6d.

Worsley.—Christian Drift of Cambridge Work.
Eight Lectures recently delivered on the Christian Bearings of Classics, Mathematics, Medicine, and Law Studies prescribed in its Charter to Downing College. By T. WORSLEY, D.D., Master of Downing College. Crown 8vo. cloth. 6s.

Wright.—David, King of Israel: Readings for the
Young. By J. WRIGHT, M.A. With Six Illustrations. Royal 16mo. cloth, gilt. 3s. 6d.

www.ingramcontent.com/pod-product-compliance
Lightning Source LLC
Chambersburg PA
CBHW020911230426
43666CB00008B/1402